JOY IN THE JOURNEY

Deseret Book Company
Salt Lake City, Utah

Appreciation is expressed to the contributors to this work for their willingness to share their thoughts and testimonies with youth. Each author accepts complete personal responsibility for the material contained within his or her chapter. There is no endorsement for this work (real or implied) by The Church of Jesus Christ of Latter-day Saints, the Church Educational System, or Brigham Young University.

Library of Congress Catalog Card Number:

Joy in the journey : favorite talks from Especially for Youth, Boys' World of Adventure, and Academy for Girls.
      p.   cm.
   Includes index.
   Summary: A compilation of talks providing advice to Latter-day Saints and emphasizing morality, religious study, and proper relationships.
   ISBN 1-57345-370-6 (pbk.)
   1. Youth—Religious life.   2. Mormon youth—Conduct of life. 3. Church of Jesus Christ of Latter-day Saints—Doctrines. [1. Church of Jesus Christ of Latter-day Saints. 2. Mormon Church. 3. Christian life.]
   BX8643.Y6J68   1998
   248.8'3—dc21   98-5748
                                                        CIP
                                                        AC

Printed in the United States of America

10 9   8   7   6   5   4   3   2   1   72082 - 6358

CONTENTS

1

JOY IN THE JOURNEY

Kim M. Peterson

There are a lot of great destinations in the world. While we may never agree on one best destination, there are several destinations that we could mutually enjoy. Maybe you would enjoy Cancun—sitting in the sun, playing in the ocean, walking in the sand, and eating good food. Perhaps you would enjoy New York City—watching Broadway shows, riding on the subway, eating from different cuisines, and walking in Central Park. We also might both enjoy hiking in Glacier National Park—breathing the crisp clean air, hiking to grandiose peaks, observing wildlife, and sitting by the campfire. This world is filled with some great places!

Regardless of our destination, one or both of us would have to travel to get there. Even if the destination is spectacular, the journey can be tedious, boring, and complicated. You may find it hard to park your car, stand in long lines in the airport, check your bags, wait for the airplane, or to listen to pages on "the white paging phone." Even after you have boarded the plane, your seat might not be completely satisfactory, the food might not be pleasant, you may be seated next to someone who bothers you, and you might not be able to complete the crossword puzzle in the in-flight magazine. Your flight could take hours! It might even include delays, layovers, and other unexpected inconveniences. Does the journey ever decrease your excitement over getting to the destination?

All of us are ticketed for the celestial kingdom. Make no mistake about the fact that your Heavenly Father created you to become like he is! You have the potential to be like the most grand being you ever comprehended. Psalm 82:6 proclaims: "I have said, Ye are gods; and all of you are children of the most High." The glory of the celestial kingdom exceeds the glory of any earthly destinations by far: "Ye shall come forth in the first resurrection . . . and shall inherit thrones, kingdoms, principalities and powers, dominions, all heights and depths . . . " (D&C 132:19). Wouldn't it be a shame to jeopardize your arrival at your heavenly destination because of some earthly diversion? What a tragedy it would be to naively conclude that the journey is too hard when it can lead to a destination that is desirable beyond comprehension.

Jesus was teaching one day in a house. Imagine yourself sitting in his presence. No doubt you would reverently listen to everything he was saying. Take an imaginary panoramic look at the house in which you would be sitting. The walls are constructed of sun-dried brick. The open windows allow the odors, sounds, and bugs to drift in from outside. The only cool air you feel comes from the gentle breezes that infrequently waft through the windows. The house is so crowded with Christ's disciples that you are sitting on the dirt floor, squished next to someone you might not know. Imagine that a tuft of thatch drops from the ceiling and lands on your head. When it happens again, you look up to see what is causing the roof to fall apart. Above you, there are four men working to cut a hole in the roof so that they might lower a man on a litter into the house. You watch curiously as the sick man is handed gently by his friends through the hole, into the room, and down to where the Savior is seated. Responding with a smile and rewarding their effort and their faith, the Savior pronounces a blessing on the palsied man, saying,

"Son, thy sins be forgiven thee" (Mark 2:5). You watch with wonder as the sick man leaps from his stretcher, thanks the Master, and walks under his own power (perhaps for the first time) out of the room, rejoicing as he goes.

One intriguing symbol in this story is the infirmity of being lame. Simply stated, the man could not walk. What a dilemma! Regardless of the faith he may have had that Christ could heal him, the man could not make his way to the Savior on his own. He needed help and had to rely on others to transport him. Each of us must also rely on others to bring us to Christ. Sadly enough, we sometimes disregard the very people who desire to help us.

The four who carried the lame man could be compared to four categories of people who are trying to help us return to Christ. What if one corner of your stretcher was held by your mom? What is your response when your mom tries to influence the things you wear? Do you resent her suggestions? I'll bet that if you asked her, she would say that she is honestly trying to help you. Maybe you have told your mother that your clothes are none of her business. In a way, you are telling her that you don't need her to help carry your stretcher even though you are lame and can't walk on your own power to Christ. Now there are only three people left to carry you.

Another corner might be carried by your bishop or some other Church leader. What is your response when Church leaders remind you that the music at dances needs to be moral, wholesome, and clean? I've frequently heard youth complain that their leaders just don't understand music. In a way, aren't you telling these leaders that you don't really need them to help carry your stretcher and that you can make it on your own even though you are lame and can't walk? What will happen to your stretcher when another person lets go? Now you only have two to carry you.

One of the last people you might admit to denying is

the prophet of God. You may never dream of telling him
that you don't need him to help carry you. What is your
response, however, when the prophet asks you to wait
until sixteen to date, or to prepare to serve missions, or to
get ready for temple marriages. I'm afraid some think they
are following the prophet if they avoid steady dating but
persist in wearing trendy fashions, listening to semimoral
music, and practicing deplorable speech patterns. By par-
ticipating in any form of immoral activity, aren't you
telling the prophet to let go? I'll bet it would be quite a jolt
if the prophet of God let go and your stretcher hit the
ground. Now you only have one carrier.

The last people you would dream of telling to let go
of your stretcher are your friends. One of the most
common lines in a teenage testimony is "I'm so grateful
for my friends because they are always there for me."
What does it mean that your friends are *always there for
you?* Does it mean that they always do or say what you
want? Does it mean that you rely on them for guidance,
strength, and support? If your friends are the only ones
you are going to allow to assist you on this journey to
Christ, they'd better be pretty strong! Picture one of your
friends working hard to drag your stretcher along the
streets of your city, in an effort to get you to the house
where the Savior is speaking. The only friends strong
enough to get you to Christ are the friends who encourage you to follow the prophet, listen to Church leaders,
and honor your parents. Such friends will urge you to
accept the help of parents, leaders, and the prophet to
help you make it to the Savior.

I've watched some "lame" teenagers tell their valiant
friends to let go. This is usually a great tragedy. If you
refuse to let anyone help, you will have to be content to
lie on your stretcher in the middle of the street.

Even when the journey is long, traveling companions
can make the journey enjoyable. Make the choice today
that you will listen to those who are trying to help you. Be

the kind of friend who will encourage others to have a good trip by obeying their parents. Become the kind of traveler who enjoys the journey as well as the destination. Even though Alma and the sons of Mosiah endured great hardships in their missionary labors, they found great joy in serving the Lord together. When they were reunited after fourteen years of separation, Mormon describes the happiness of Ammon (one of the sons of Mosiah): "Now the joy of Ammon was so great even that he was full; yea, he was swallowed up in the joy of his God, even to the exhausting of his strength . . . Behold, this is joy which none receiveth save it be the truly penitent and humble seeker of happiness" (Alma 27:17–18).

In my interactions with the youth of the Church, I have had the opportunity to meet some valiant travelers. These great souls seem to be able to enjoy the journey even when the road is rough, the trail is steep, the layovers are long, or the delays are unexpected. They are able to give some wonderful hints on how to make the journey joyous. While their stories are simple, we can learn much from them about how to be a "seeker of happiness."

I met one young man who was particularly tempted by pornography. Despite all of his attempts to avoid it, he failed. Satan just seemed to place it in front of him. He once told me that he was afraid of trying to avoid it because every time he tried, the problem just seemed to get worse. He said that he was hopeful that if he asked his bishop for help, the temptations wouldn't be so strong. Instead, he said he was tempted even more. I encouraged him to keep in touch with his bishop and to make his problem a matter of prayer. Several days later, he recounted to me an experience he had while reading his scriptures. He said that he was reading in 2 Nephi 4 and found that Nephi also seemed to have struggles because he exclaims: "O wretched man that I am! Yea, my heart sorroweth because of my flesh; my soul grieveth because of mine iniquities! I am encompassed about, because of the

temptations and the sins which do so easily beset me. And
when I desire to rejoice, my heart groaneth because of my
sins; nevertheless, I know in whom I have trusted" (vv.
17–19).

By the report of this young man, when he depended on
his own strength and determination, he failed; but when
he trusted in God, he was able to resist the lure of pornography. What a great hint on how to have a joyous journey:
if we try to do it on our own, we will be miserable, but if
through prayer and scripture study we make the Lord our
traveling companion, we will not only make it to our destination, but we will enjoy the trip.

I know of one young woman who had to endure the
horrible trial of abuse. Even after she had been taken out
of her house and removed from the abusive situation, she
was faced with loneliness and an overwhelming feeling of
rejection. Though others who have been abused often
have feelings of bitterness toward their abusers, this young
woman seemed to be able to forgive and function quite
well, despite her experiences. When I asked her about how
she was able to do so, she said that she thought of Christ.
Even after he was nailed to the cross and had endured
tremendous ridicule by those who should have wor-
shipped him, the first words out of his mouth were still,
"Father, forgive them . . . " (Luke 23:34). She continued by
explaining that if Christ could forgive his tormentors, she
felt it was her responsibility to forgive also (see D&C
64:9–11). This is another important traveling hint: follow
the Savior's example.

I know of another young man who was quite popular at
school, where he excelled in both sports and academics.
He had a promising future playing high school basketball,
but he decided practice demanded too much of his time.
He wanted to serve a mission and had determined to
follow the prophet's counsel and pay his own way. The
time required by both school and sports made it impossible to hold a job and begin saving for his mission. When
he tried to explain why he was quitting the team, his

coach tried to persuade him otherwise by telling him that God had given him a talent for playing basketball and that God wanted him to use his talents to play. Rather than give in to the pressure of the coach, the young man explained that he believed in the principle of sacrifice. He was willing to give up basketball for something more important.

Ignoring the pressure to do otherwise, this faithful young man followed the counsel of a prophet, going against a world that values games over spiritual things. In an effort to explain his motivation, the young man quoted D&C 128:22: "Go forward and not backward. Courage, brethren; and on, on to the victory!" He said that this scripture had given him the courage to do what was right. What a great traveling hint: we can derive courage from the scriptures.

It takes faith to embark on any journey—especially when we are traveling to a strange or unknown destination. Travelers are required to believe in a destination that they may never have seen. It also takes hope to plan a trip. It is the hope of arrival that can strengthen faith during the journey. Moroni teaches that hope and faith are closely related: "Wherefore, if a man have faith he must needs have hope; for without faith there cannot be any hope" (Moroni 7:42).

Having even the hope of arrival at a destination requires faith. Travelers must believe their destination exists and that getting there is worth the trip before they can ever begin to hope to arrive. Maybe the hope of spending a vacation in Cancun, New York, or Glacier National Park comes from listening to the experiences others have had at those places. Hope can also be inspired by looking at pictures of the destination or similar locations. If you've been on a beach in Hawaii, you might hope for a similar experience in Cancun. If you've seen a stage play, you may expect that seeing the play on Broadway would be a great experience. If you've been hiking in Yosemite, you can hope to have a similar experience in Glacier. Ether teaches us that hope comes from faith and "maketh an anchor to the souls of men, which would make them sure and stead-fast, always abounding in good works, being led to glorify God" (Ether 12:4).

Faith comes from hope and hope comes from faith! (see Moroni 7:40–42). In our example of finding "joy in the journey," we might conclude that moving closer to God can increase our hope or anticipation of arriving one day in the presence of God. We might also conclude that our hope of coming unto Christ can inspire us to travel more joyfully. One of the pinnacle doctrines of the Book of Mormon was taught by Lehi to his son Jacob: "Adam fell that men might be; and men are, that they might have joy" (2 Nephi 2:25). Apparently, the only way we could progress toward becoming like God was to leave his pres-ence. We owe our existence to Adam and Eve who decided to partake of the tree of knowledge of good and evil. The purpose of our existence, the purpose of this life, the meaning of our creation, is to have joy! That joy is not just available in the celestial kingdom but can be experienced in our journey back to God's presence. Eve concluded that were it not for their transgression, they "never should have known good and evil, and the joy of our redemption, and the eternal life which God giveth unto all the obedi-ent" (Moses 5:11).

Regardless of your means of travel, the anticipation of reaching the destination can inspire joy in the journey. Whether the journey is easy or the road is difficult, you can have joy in traveling. Faith, hope, and an eye single to the glory of God (reading scripture) can make even a tedious journey enjoyable. After being separated from their families for some time, Sidney Rigdon and Joseph Smith were comforted by the Lord with these words: "Therefore, continue your journey and let your hearts rejoice; for behold, and lo, I am with you even unto the end" (D&C 100:12). I would guess that any journey under-taken with Christ would be enjoyable.

As you read the chapters in this book, identify ways to

come unto Christ. Find an opportunity to underline the scriptures quoted. Apply the stories to your own life. Look for opportunities to follow the counsel contained in each chapter. As you do, you will also find increased joy in your journey back to your Heavenly Father.

Kim Peterson is a seminary and institute instructor in the Denver, Colorado, area. He loves to ski and has been employed as a ski instructor during the winter months. Kim also enjoys cooking a variety of "Oriental dishes." He and his wife, Terri, have one son and one daughter. Kim has a goal never to become an "R.M." (Ask him what he means by that when you get a chance.)

2

ACT I:
THE PREMORTAL LIFE

Curtis L. Jacobs

W hy?" my three-year-old adorable daughter asked. I tried to explain. My attempt was unsuccessful. Out would come the same word again, "Why?" "Why, Daddy?" One of the first words children seem to learn is *why?* Even worse, one of the next phrases they learn is *why not?*

Speaking to thousands of seminary and institute personnel in the Church Education System, President Boyd K. Packer told the story of a parent who once got after his child by saying, "Why on earth did you do such a thing?" The child responded, "If I'd had a 'why,' I wouldn't have done it" (CES Symposium, 1993). All of us like to know why. Why do I have to go to school? Why should I say my prayers? Why are we commanded to do some things and not others? Why should I read the scriptures? Good questions all, and most can be answered if we are willing to remember some basic principles. By remembering these principles, we can really find "joy in the journey." So, let's get going.

A few years ago President Packer spoke to young adults all over the country (and beyond) via satellite. His talk was entitled "The Play and the Plan" (CES Fireside, May 7,

1995). Those of you who have been members of the Church very long have all seen "The Plan of Salvation" diagrammed on a chalkboard: A circle in the top left corner for the premortal existence, a line (the veil), another circle (earth), another line (death), a bar (resurrection and judgment), and finally three circles (the three degrees of glory). In his talk, President Packer said that "a knowledge of the plan . . . , even in outline form, can give young minds a 'why'."

President Packer likened the Plan of Salvation to a three-act play. ACT 1 is entitled "Premortal Life." The scriptures describe this act as our "First Estate." ACT 2, from birth to the time of resurrection, is the "Second Estate." ACT 3 is life after death, or eternal life.

This chapter will deal with ACT 1.

ACT 1

One of the most important "whys?" we all need answered is, "Why am I here on earth?" For centuries mankind has tried to come up with an answer to that question. However, because of the restoration of the gospel we have a complete understanding of our purpose here. This knowledge comes to us because of what we know about our premortal life. In fact, in another talk, President Packer indicates that we can't truly make sense of mortality without a knowledge of the premortal life. "When we understand the doctrine of premortal life, then things fit together and make sense" (*Ensign,* November 1983, 18). The fact that we believe we had life before this one sets us apart from the rest of the Christian world. If we truly understand ACT 1, it can help us in ACT 2 and ACT 3.

Most of you have probably seen (even several times) the Church film, *Man's Search for Happiness.* In the film you hear the following quote:

> *Our birth is but a sleep and a forgetting:*
> *The soul that rises with us, our life's star,*

> *Hath had elsewhere its setting,*
> *And cometh from afar;*
> *Not in entire forgetfulness,*
> *And not in utter nakedness,*
> *But trailing clouds of glory do we come*
> *From God, who is our home.*
>
> (William Wordsworth, *"Ode: Intimations of*
> *Immortality from Recollections of Early Childhood"*)

Yes, we came from God, our Heavenly Father. So what do you remember about ACT 1, the premortal life? Now I realize that some of you are thinking, *real funny,* I can't remember anything! Doesn't this Jacobs guy know about the veil? Fair enough, so what have you been taught?

First off, you and I are literally, and I mean *literally,* the spiritually begotten children of divine parents. Back in 1909 (yes, that's a few years before you were around these mortal parts), the First Presidency said: "All men and women are in the similitude of the universal Father and Mother, and are literally the sons and daughters of Deity." What a genealogy we have! We all come from the most royal lineage possible. We are truly children of God. With the knowledge of that one simple doctrine we also can determine what we have the potential to become.

I have written about this before, but I think it bears repeating. Now, I'm about to ask some hard questions, so you might want to sit down. What does a puppy have the potential to become? What does a kitten have the potential to become? A fawn? A colt? A calf? (How many do you think you got right? The correct answers are: dog, cat, deer, horse, cow.) Can you see the point? The offspring of "whatever" has the potential to become like its parents! Can you even imagine a greater potential than the one you and I have? So the next time you sing, "I am a child of God," it should remind you of your potential.

According to prophets past and present, we lived in the

premortal world for eons of time. (Now exactly how long an eon is, I can't say, but know this: it's a lot more than the years you'll have in ACT 2!)

So what in the world, actually, what in *heaven,* did we do? As spirits we had our moral agency. We had many choices given us. We could choose to develop certain talents and characteristics. What talents and abilities do you think you developed there?

Ever heard of Mozart? He started playing the piano pretty early in life (like about age four), and he wrote scores of music by the time he was eight! How come? Could it be he started learning music a few hundred (or thousand) years earlier? Elder Bruce R. McConkie put it this way, "Having their agency, all the spirits of men, while yet in the Eternal Presence, developed aptitudes, talents, capacities, and abilities of every sort, kind, and degree. During the long expanse of life which then was, an infinite variety of talents and abilities came into being. . . . The whole house of Israel, known and segregated out from their fellows, was inclined toward spiritual things" (*The Mortal Messiah, Book 1* [1979], 23). Can you see how a knowledge of ACT 1 can help us understand, at least in part, why people can be so very different, even at a very early age? Again, I ask, what talents, etc. did you develop before you were even born? Did you know you might have been developing the talent of spirituality long before you got to earth? Keep it up!

As spirits, however, we could only learn and develop so far. The time came when we were all brought together in a big "family home evening" in heaven. (Can you imagine being in charge of the refreshments?) In this setting we were taught about a plan. It is often referred to as "The Plan of Salvation." It was devised by our Heavenly Father and provided a means by which, if we followed it, we would become more like him. In fact, that is the primary purpose of the plan.

This plan of God's provided several exciting new things for us, including the following: There would be an earth created for us to one day live upon. There would be agency allowed on this earth. There would be the Fall of Man. This would bring mortality and death into the world. There would be opposition in all things, so that we could prove whether or not we would be willing to choose the good over the evil. President Spencer W. Kimball has written, "We knew before we were born that we were coming to the earth for bodies and experience and that we would have joys and sorrows, ease and pain, comforts and hardships, health and sickness, successes and disappointments, and we knew also that after a period of life we would die. We accepted all these eventualities with a glad heart, eager to accept both the favorable and unfavorable. We eagerly accepted the chance to come earthward even though it might be for only a day or a year" (Spencer W. Kimball, *Faith Precedes the Miracle* [1973], 106).

Elder Neal A. Maxwell has stated, "To what degree we were permitted, before coming here, to see all the outcomes and the risks of mortality, such as war and poverty, we presently know not. A *just* God surely would have let us understand sufficiently about that upon which we are soon to embark. However, with whatever measure of understanding we then had, some 'shouted for joy,' a stirring reaction that ought to tell us enough in terms of our perceptions then, when we had some added perspective" (*Even As I Am* [1982], 107).

There may have been something else we did prior to coming to earth. Elder Maxwell, quoting Elder Orson Hyde, has suggested that while still in ACT 1, we may have made certain agreements. We may have even signed with our own hands some document saying we would accomplish those things. Then, those documents could be brought forth when we rise from the dead and we could thereby be judged according to the things that were written (see *Ensign,* February 1979, 72).

Our Father in Heaven knew that this earth life would be a great testing place. Because of the temptations that would be allowed to be present on earth, he knew that we all (save one) would make mistakes, sin, and fall short of perfection here in mortality. The divine plan required one to be sent as a Savior and Redeemer. The Father asked for a volunteer. His Firstborn in the Spirit, Jesus (known in the premortal world as Jehovah), willingly accepted the opportunity of becoming our Savior with five simple words, "Here am I, send me." By volunteering to be our Savior under the Father's plan, he was willing to come to earth, be completely perfect, pay the price of the sins and suffer the pains of men. He would suffer and die that we might live again and be able to return to live with our Heavenly Father. His was the ultimate sacrifice.

Because of the Savior's atonement, we knew that we could repent of the sins we would commit. We understood that we would have the opportunity to accept the gospel, either on earth or in the spirit world following physical death. The gospel would give us the necessary commandments and ordinances required to return and live with God through the Atonement. We also knew there would one day come a Final Judgment. We would be judged on what we had done—how well we had followed the plan. Those who kept their "second estate" (ACT 2) would have glory added upon their heads for ever and ever. (Now that's a LONG time.)

Those of us who kept this second estate would finally reach our greatest potential. Remember what a kitten can become? One thing for sure, when it comes to Judgment Day, there won't be any successful unrepentant sinners! The righteous will have "a perfect knowledge of their enjoyment, and their righteousness, being clothed with purity, yea, even with the robe of righteousness" (2 Nephi 9:14). The wicked? Well, have you ever had a bad day? They will stand before God, having a "bright recollection of all [their] guilt" (Alma 11:43). Personally, I like the first option.

There was another, however, who had different ideas. His name was Lucifer. "Here am I, send me, I will be thy son, and I will redeem all mankind, that one soul shall not be lost, and surely I will do it, wherefore give me thine [Heavenly Father's] honor," he proudly declared (Moses 4:1). What "I" trouble! What arrogance! He would destroy our agency (see Moses 4:3) and then try and take the glory of God to himself! Lucifer's plan wouldn't really require a "Savior" to pay for sin. Under his plan sin wouldn't be allowed. He wanted "all the gain, but none of the pain!"

There was war in heaven. You and I fought against Lucifer. We fought for the plan of our Heavenly Father! In ACT 1 we showed who we were really for: our Heavenly Father and our Savior Jesus Christ.

Lucifer became Satan. He with his host of devils would be denied physical bodies. They would try to destroy the Father's plan. Satan would still try to have it his way. His plan is just the opposite of Heavenly Father's, and it is to make all men miserable like unto himself (see 2 Nephi 2:27). Talk about the ultimate "misery likes company" person. What a loser!

We understood there what the plan was all about. We could hardly wait for our turn on earth. However, in coming to earth, we would have a veil drawn across our memory. That loss of memory gives us a clean start. It is ideal for the test; it leaves us free to make choices. Many of these choices must be made on faith alone. See, if we could remember ACT 1, it would be too easy. I remember when my dad would ask me to mow the lawn. If I knew he was right there watching me, I'd get it done quick. But, if he left, then I could decide on my own to obey or not. Of course, I learned that obedience was the only way to go. The veil does sort of the same thing for us. We have left our Father's presence and now can choose to obey or not. However, since we agreed to the conditions of mortality, the veil does not alter what was agreed to there in ACT 1—Just as a doctor doesn't wake up a person in the middle of surgery to ask again if the surgery should be continued. Agreeing to come here to earth was an irrevocable decision (see *Ensign,* February 1979, 70).

Having an understanding that we lived with our heavenly parents as their spirit children prior to coming to earth can be of great benefit here during ACT 2. If we will remember the purpose of earth life was clear to us there, it will help us here. We knew then that the Lord's commandments were given to help us become more like him, not as some sort of punishment. God loves us. He gave us this plan. We accepted it. We have a Savior willing to forgive us and lead us. We followed them there, let's continue to follow them here. "We chose not to follow Lucifer once: let us not go back on that decision now!" (Neal A. Maxwell, *Even As I Am,* 35).

Elder David B. Haight has said: "Though the world is becoming more wicked, the youth of Christ's church can become more righteous *if they understand who they are,* understand the blessings available, and understand the promises God has made to those who are righteous, who believe, who endure" (*Ensign,* January 1974, 40; emphasis in original).

If you'll remember who you are, where you came from, and live the way you know you should, you will have joy in the journey here in ACT 2, and perfect joy in ACT 3.

I testify that you have incredible potential. In ACT 1 you chose correctly. You were wonderful. You have a divine destiny. God's plan of happiness, versus Satan's plan of misery, sounds like a pretty easy choice to me.

Curtis Jacobs was born in Ogden, Utah, and served a mission in Anchorage, Alaska. He and his wife, Jolene, have four very hyper kids. He plays a wicked game of racquetball, probably because of his experience as a gymnast. He received his bachelor's degree from Utah State University and a master's degree from Northern Arizona University. Currently he is an instructor at the institute of religion in Logan, Utah.

3

ACT II:
MORTALITY

Randall C. Bird

As a young boy I remember traveling with my family from Idaho to New York City to attend the World's Fair. I was in awe as I attended the fair and its many pavilions and booths and marveled at the number of religions that had space at the fair. I visited most of those booths and was impressed with the messages of inspiration given there, especially the message and feeling I received at the Mormon Pavilion. I watched with real interest a beautiful film presented there entitled, *Man's Search for Happiness*. This film depicted the Father's plan of salvation and asked three vitally important questions: Where did I come from? Why am I here? and Where am I going after this life? Can you imagine my joy when several years later I received a mission call to serve in the Eastern States Mission with headquarters in New York City. There, I met and taught people who were searching for the meaning of life, and as I sat in their homes, they specifically wanted to know the answers to the three questions mentioned above.

In the chapter in this book by Curtis Jacobs, you can read about where we came from. For my chapter of the book, I have been asked to write about mortality and the meaning of life. In his discussion of the purposes of mortality, President Boyd K. Packer of the Quorum of the Twelve Apostles has referred to this life as Act II in our eternal existence. I hope that what follows will help you understand the purpose of mortality and answer the question "Why Am I Here?"

AGENCY

The proper exercise of our moral agency is essential to becoming like God (see 2 Nephi 2:14–16). Elder Bruce R. McConkie said, "Agency underlies all things—all advancement, all progression, even existence itself. It is based on the presence of opposites between which a choice must be made. If there were no opposites, there would be nothing. 'It must needs be, that there is an opposition in all things,' Lehi said, 'If not so . . . righteousness could not be brought to pass, neither wickedness, neither holiness nor misery, neither good nor bad.' Then, to show why all this is so, Lehi reasoned, with divine insight and logic, in this way: If there were no opposites, and thus no agency, 'all things must needs be a compound in one.' That is, things would be both good and bad, hot and cold, light and dark at one and the same time, a thing that is impossible, as Lehi will show. 'Wherefore, if it should be one body it must needs remain as dead,' he continues, 'having no life neither death, nor corruption nor incorruption, happiness nor misery, neither sense nor insensibility.' Again, this is something that could not be. But assuming it to be so, Lehi reaches this conclusion: 'Wherefore, it must needs have been created for a thing of naught; wherefore there would have been no purpose in the end of its creation. Wherefore, this thing must needs destroy the wisdom of God and his eternal purposes, and also the power, and the mercy, and the justice of God.'

"Thus, if men were not accountable for their own sins, if they were not agents unto themselves, the very purpose of creation and existence would vanish away and the

plans and designs of God would fail. 'And if ye shall say
there is no law, ye shall also say there is no sin,' the divine
reasoning continues. 'If ye shall say there is no sin, ye shall
also say there is no righteousness. And if there be no righteousness there be no happiness. And if there be no righteousness nor happiness there be no punishment nor misery. And if these things are not there is no God. And if
there is no God we are not, neither the earth; for there
could have been no creation of things, neither to act nor
to be acted upon; wherefore, all things must have van-
ished away.' Such is the logic and reasoning of heaven.
Opposites, agency, justice, rewards and punishments—all
these are and must be part of the eternal plan. Without
them, nothing would or could exist" (*A New Witness for
the Articles of Faith* [1985], 90–91).

There are, however, some consequences to granting
man the opportunity to choose. Agency is essential to our
growth, but it is inevitable that man will not always
choose correctly, "for all have sinned, and come short of
the glory of God" (Romans 3:23). Were agency all that was
provided, we would all be condemned. But in the "plan"
he presented to his children in the premortal council, a
merciful Father provided a remedy for the sins we would
all commit.

PHYSICAL CREATION

The physical creation of the heavens and the earth, and
all things therein, was an essential step in helping us
become like our Father in Heaven (see Moses 1:33–39;
Abraham 3:24–26). When God created the earth, he pronounced it "very good" (Moses 2:31) and a place of beauty
and abundance (see Genesis 1:1–2:25; Moses 2:1–31;
3:7–25; Abraham 4:1–5:21).

President Boyd K. Packer taught, "An earth was then
organized (Abr. 5:4). Adam and Eve in a paradisiacal state
were the first man and first woman (see Moses 1:34; 3:7;
4:26; 6:3–10, 22, 59). They were married eternally (see
Moses 3:23–24) and were given commandments. They

were in a state of innocence and knew no sin (2 Nephi 2:23)" ("The Play and the Plan," 4).

On one occasion, after Moses had been shown some of God's numberless creations, he asked two questions: (1) What is the purpose of your creations? and (2) By what power did you make them? The answer to the first question is stated in Moses 1:39, where God explains his purposes. In answer to the second question, the Lord told Moses that he would not explain everything concerning all his creations, but that he would explain some things having to do with this earth only. This included the often overlooked truth that all things were created by God's "Only Begotten" who is Jesus Christ (see Moses 1:33). Then in Moses 2–3, God gave Moses some additional details concerning the creation of this earth. You'll want to read those chapters as you study further the Creation.

THE FALL AND MORTALITY

The fall of Adam and Eve was the step leading to mortality in the "great plan of happiness." It is important to note that Adam *chose* to become mortal and leave the garden. Had they been forced out of the garden, or placed in a fallen world to begin with, they would have been inclined to blame God for all their challenges, sorrows, and sins. Elder John A. Widtsoe taught, "The choice that they made raises Adam and Eve to pre-eminence among all who have come on earth. The Lord's plan was given life by them. They are indeed, as far as this earth is concerned, our loving father and mother. The 'Fall' and the consequent redeeming act of Jesus became the most glorious events in the history of mankind. . . . Adam and Eve rise to the position of helpers in initiating the divine purpose on earth. They become partners with the Lord in making eternal joy possible for the hosts of heaven" (*Evidences and Reconciliations* [1960], 194–95).

The Fall brought about the conditions of mortality, including spiritual and physical death (see 2 Nephi

2:19–25; Alma 42:1–10). Mortal life on earth is essential to becoming like God. It provides us with the opportunity to gain a physical body and to learn the lessons of godhood by having the freedom to choose to follow the counsel of God or the enticements of Satan (see Alma 42:1–12; Moses 5:9–12). It is by the choices we make that we "prove" ourselves (see Abraham 3:25).

Referring to his metaphor of life as a three-act play, President Packer gave his counsel about our mortal condition, "As part of the eternal plan, the memory of our premortal life, Act I, is covered with a veil. Since you enter mortality at the beginning of Act II with no recollection of Act I, it is little wonder that it is difficult to understand what is going on.

"That loss of memory gives us a clean start. It is ideal for the test; it secures our individual agency and leaves us free to make choices. Many of them must be made on faith alone. Even so, we carry with us some whispered knowledge of our premortal life and our status as offspring of immortal parents.

"You were born in innocence, for 'every spirit of man was innocent in the beginning' (D&C 93:38). And you have an inborn sense of right and wrong, for the scriptures tell us in the Book of Mormon, we 'are instructed sufficiently that [we] know good from evil' (2 Nephi 2:5).

"If you expect to find only ease and peace and bliss during Act II, you surely will be frustrated. You will understand little of what is going on and why things are permitted to be as they are.

"Remember this! The line **'And they all lived happily ever after'** is never written into the second act. That line belongs in the third act when the mysteries are solved and everything is put right.

"Until you have a broad perspective of the eternal nature of this great drama, you won't make much sense out of the inequities in life. Some are born with so little and others with so much, some in poverty, with handicaps, with pain, with suffering, premature death even of innocent children. There are the brutal, unforgiving forces of nature and the brutality of man to man. We've seen a lot of that recently.

"Do not suppose that God willfully causes that, which for his own purposes, he permits. When you know the plan and purpose of it all, even these things will manifest a loving Father in Heaven.

"There exists something of a script for this great play, the drama of the ages.

"That script, as you should already know, is the scriptures, the revelations. Read them, study them.

"The scriptures speak the truth. From them you can learn enough about all three acts to get your bearings and get direction in your life. They reveal that, 'Ye were also in the beginning with the Father; that which is Spirit, even the Spirit of truth; and truth is knowledge of things as they are, and as they were, and as they are to come' (D&C 93:23–24): Act I, Act II, and Act III.

"You can learn of things as they were, as they actually are, not just as they appear to be, and you can learn of things as they are to come. What happens to you after the curtain comes down on this second act of mortal life, we take on faith. Each of us writes our own ending to Act II.

"Now, here you are on stage in Act II of this eternal drama, your own second estate.

"You live in the last days, a dispensation of intense testing and unequaled opportunity. Paul the Apostle wrote a remarkable prophecy to young Timothy. He said, 'In the last days perilous times shall come' (2 Timothy 3:1). He described our day in accurate detail.

"He wrote of men becoming 'lovers of their own selves' (2 Timothy 3:2). He spoke of disobedience to parents, of 'despisers of those who are good' (2 Timothy 3:3). He even saw those who 'without natural affection' (2 Timothy 3:3) could abuse little children, and those who now rally in protest for the abandonment of those standards without which civilization will not endure.

"Now when enough people protest limits on conduct,

the limits are moved farther out and behavior that was once prohibited is reclassified as moral, legal, and socially acceptable, and people rally and protest to make it so. The bonds of marriage and kinship are seen as bondage rather than as sacred ties. The home, the family, absolutely critical to the Plan, are now besieged. And are on stage in the center of it all.

"Just as the air you breathe may expose you to deadly virus, the thoughts you think may introduce spiritual diseases which, if untreated, may be spiritually fatal.

"But Paul's prophecy of the perilous last days include an antidote, the immunization, which can protect, even cure you. After describing those who are 'ever learning, and never able to come to the knowledge of the truth' (2 Timothy 3:7), he counseled, 'But continue thou in the things which thou hast learned and hast been assured of, knowing of whom thou has learned them.' Know who is teaching you.

"'And that from a child thou hast known the holy scriptures, which are able to make thee wise unto salvation through faith which is in Christ Jesus.'

"'All scripture is given by inspiration of God, and is profitable for doctrine, for reproof, for correction, for instruction in righteousness' (2 Timothy 3:14–16)" ("The Play and the Plan," 3–5).

THE MISSION OF THE CHURCH AND THE PRINCIPLES AND ORDINANCES OF THE GOSPEL

The fall of Adam and Eve was not a mistake or a surprise. Had they not chosen to become mortal, neither they nor the rest of Heavenly Father's children could have progressed to become like God (see 2 Nephi 2:22–25). Thus the Fall was a necessary part of the plan, but it does have some negative consequences from which we need to be saved. The gospel of Jesus Christ provides a way for all mankind to be redeemed from the Fall and brought back into the presence of God to be like him (see 2 Nephi 3:10–21; Mosiah 3:19). If we refuse to follow the plan and do not accept the atonement of Jesus Christ, we cannot be redeemed and perfected (see Mosiah 2:36–39; 4:1–12). In every dispensation, Jesus Christ has sent prophets to teach His gospel to God's children on earth. The Church of Jesus Christ has been established in these latter days to invite all to come unto Christ, by proclaiming the gospel to the world, perfecting the Saints, and redeeming the dead (see Amos 3:7; Ephesians 4:11–15; D&C 1:4–23).

President Packer said, "Eve, beguiled by Satan (see Moses 4:6, 19), transgressed and was to be cast out of the Garden. Adam chose to obey the first commandment to multiply and replenish the earth. Adam and Eve were subject to the Fall which introduced mortality to the earth (see Moses 2:28; 3:17; 4:13; Alma 12:22). Adam and Eve became the first parents of the family of all the earth (2 Nephi 21:20).

"Angels were sent to reveal to Adam the eternal plan of redemption (see Moses 5:4–9; 6:48–62) and an atonement was wrought by Jesus Christ. Through the Atonement the effects of the Fall, mortal death and spiritual death, could both be overcome (see Alma 42:7–9; Helaman 14:16–18). Christ unconditionally provided a resurrection for all mankind and thereby overcame physical death (see Helaman 14:15).

"But to overcome spiritual death, which is separation from God, requires that we be obedient to the laws and ordinances of the gospel of Jesus Christ (see AF 1:3; TPJS, 48).

"These principles and ordinances were instituted before the foundation of the world. They are not to be altered or changed. All must be saved by the same requirements (TPJS, 308, 358–60, 367). The priesthood administers the ordinances of salvation (*TPJS,* 158). The keys of the priesthood control the use of the priesthood (see D&C 27:12–13; 110; *TPJS,* 157)" ("The Play and the Plan," 4). Those who do not have the opportunity in mortality to receive the gospel and the saving ordinances are also provided for (see 2 Nephi 9:25).

THE ATONEMENT

Because of the fall of Adam all mankind is faced with several serious problems: we will all die (physical death); we are all cut off from the presence of God (spiritual death) and cannot get back on our own; and we live in a world of toil, sin, and sorrow. The atonement of Jesus Christ provides for the resurrection of all men with an immortal physical body, thus overcoming physical death. Through the Atonement we can also be cleansed from personal sins and changed from our fallen condition to return to God, thus overcoming spiritual death. Read and study the following references: 2 Nephi 2:5–10; 9:4–14, 19–27; Alma 7:11–13; 12:32–34; 34:9–16; 42:11–28; D&C 19:16–19; Articles of Faith 1:3. Also because of the Atonement, the earth will be returned to its paradisiacal state (see Articles of Faith 1:10). No ordinary man could have brought about the Resurrection and atoned for the sins of all mankind. Only one who had power over death and the power of a sinless life could have done so. In short, it required the sacrifice of a God (see John 10:17–18; Alma 34:9–14; D&C 45:4).

Agency, the Creation, the Fall, the Atonement, and ordinances are all part of mortality. After we finish Act II or our second estate, we will have the opportunity to continue in the Father's plan by entering Act III (which is discussed by Todd Parker in another chapter of this book). It should be remembered that what we do in Act II will have eternal consequences for better or worse in Act III. This period of mortal probation gives us great opportunity to walk by faith, receive the ordinances necessary for exaltation, and by obedience to those laws and ordinances, enter back into the presence of the Lord. What a blessing it is to know that we are children of a loving Father in Heaven, who has provided a way for us to return to his presence. May the Lord truly bless us to understand who we are, where we came from, why we're here, and where we're going.

Randall C. Bird was born in Blackfoot, Idaho. He is married to Carla Aikele of Arco, Idaho, and they have six children, four girls and two boys. Randall served in the Eastern States Mission and then obtained bachelor's and master's degrees from BYU. He is currently stake president of the Layton Utah East Stake. Besides working as an assistant football coach and head track coach in high school athletics, he taught seminary in Idaho for twenty years and is currently manager of seminary curriculum for the Church Educational System in Salt Lake City. For the past twenty-two years he has been directing and lecturing at BYU's EFY programs.

4

ACT III:
LIFE AFTER DEATH

Todd Parker

Each year thousands of people visit Temple Square and tour the visitors center there.

Many visitors watch the Church-produced movie, *Man's Search for Happiness,* narrated by Elder Richard L. Evans. The movie depicts a family with young children and a grandfather who lives with them. Eventually the grandfather dies. As the family stands by the snowy grave of their beloved grandfather, Richard L. Evans's comforting voice says: "Like every member of the human race, you were born and you must die. Your birth is a matter of record; you take it for granted. But death, that uncertain door that leads ahead, has been for man an awesome mystery. Life's greatest test comes with the death of a loved one; and without faith in the immortality of the soul, the separation of death looms forever comfortless."

To help us understand what to expect after this life, President Boyd K. Packer addressed the youth of the Church and compared life to a three-act play. Act I is the premortal existence; Act II, mortality; and Act III, life after death (see "The Play and the Plan." May 7, 1995, CES Satellite Broadcast). He explained that by understanding this plan we can gain a better perspective of our purpose in life and what to expect in the life to come. To help broaden our perspective for "Act III," we will consider questions often asked by both youth and adult members of the Church. The answers to these questions will be based on passages of scripture and statements that have been made by the General Authorities.

In the postmortal world, there are two major divisions: the spirit world and the Resurrection. We'll begin first with questions about the spirit world.

WHAT HAPPENS AT DEATH?

From the Doctrine and Covenants we learn that "the spirit and the body are the soul of man" (D&C 88:15). James, the Lord's brother, wrote in the New Testament, "The body without the spirit is dead" (James 2:26). At death, the body and the spirit separate. The body returns to the earth, but the spirit enters a new realm called the spirit world. In the movie, *Man's Search for Happiness,* Elder Evans described it this way: "After death, though your mortal body lies in the earth, you, your spirit self, being eternal, continues to live. Your memory of this life will remain with you and the knowledge of your life before birth will be restored. Like coming out of a darkened room into the light, through death you will emerge into a place of reawakening and find loved ones, waiting to welcome you."

WHERE IS THE SPIRIT WORLD?

Brigham Young asked this question himself and answered it this way:

"Where is the Spirit World?—Is the spirit world here? It is not beyond the sun, but is on this earth that was organized for the people that have lived and that do and will live upon it. . . .

"When you lay down this tabernacle, where are you going? Into the spiritual world. Are you going into Abraham's bosom [meaning the presence of God]? No, not anywhere nigh there but into the spirit world. Where is the spirit world? It is right here. Do the good and evil spirits go together? Yes, they do. Do they both inhabit one kingdom? Yes, they do. Do they go to the sun? No. Do they go beyond the boundaries of the organized earth? No, they do not. . . .

"If the Lord would permit it, and it was his will that it should be done, you could see the spirits that have departed from this world, as plainly as you now see bodies with your natural eyes" (*Discourses of Brigham Young,* sel. John A. Widtsoe [1946], 376–77).

Elder Parley P. Pratt wrote of the spirit world: "It is here on the very planet where we were born, or in other words, the earth and other planets of a like sphere have their inward or spiritual spheres as well as their outward, or temporal. The one is peopled by temporal tabernacles, and the other by spirits. A veil is drawn between the one sphere and the other whereby all the objects in the spiritual sphere are rendered invisible to those in the temporal" (*Key to the Science of Theology* [1978], 81).

Some people mistakenly believe that at death we enter the presence of God. This is not the case. As resurrected beings, God and Christ dwell in a celestial world apart from this one. Heber C. Kimball said: "As for my going into the immediate presence of God when I die, I do not expect it, but I expect to go into the world of spirits and associate with my brethren, and preach the Gospel in the spiritual world, and prepare myself in every necessary way to receive my body again, and then enter through the wall into the celestial world. I never shall come into the presence of my Father and God until I have received my resurrected body, neither will any other person" (*Journal of Discourses,* 3:112–13).

The postmortal spirit world is a place of residence for those who have died and are awaiting resurrection when their spirits and bodies will unite again. Life in the spirit world is an intermediate condition between earth life and life as a resurrected being.

WHAT IS IT LIKE IN THE SPIRIT WORLD?

The Lord revealed to Joseph Smith: "There is no such thing as immaterial matter. All spirit is matter, but it is more fine or pure, and can only be discerned by purer eyes; we cannot see it; but when our bodies are purified we shall see that it is all matter" (D&C 131:7–8).

The spirit world is very similar to this world but in another dimension. Although it's here on this earth and we cannot see it with our natural eyes, it exists. It has the kinds of things we have in the world. In that world there are spirit bushes, trees, lakes, buildings, flowers, etc. Brigham Young said, "Spirits are just as familiar with spirits as bodies are with bodies, though spirits are composed of matter so refined as not to be tangible to this coarser organization" (*Discourses of Brigham Young*, 379).

Once when he was very ill, Jedediah Grant's spirit left his body. President Heber C. Kimball later went to visit him and recalled what Brother Grant told him in these words: "He said to me, 'Brother Heber, I have been into the spirit world two nights in succession, and, of all the dreads that ever came across me, the worst was to have to again return to my body, though I had to do it.' But 'O,' says he, 'the order and government that were there! When in the spirit world, I saw the order of righteous men and women. . . . ' He said that the people he there saw were organized in family capacities; and . . . all were organized and in perfect harmony. . . .

"He saw the righteous gathered together in the spirit world, and there were no wicked spirits among them. He saw his wife; she was the first person that came to him. He saw many that he knew, but did not have conversation with any except his wife Caroline. She came to him, and he said that she looked beautiful and had their little child, that died on the Plains, in her arms, and said, 'Mr. Grant, here is little Margaret; you know that the wolves ate her up, but it did not hurt her; here she is all right.' . . .

"He also spoke of the buildings he saw there, remarking

that the Lord gave Solomon wisdom and poured gold and silver into his hands that he might display his skill and ability, and said that the temple erected by Solomon was much inferior to the most ordinary buildings he saw in the spirit world.

"'In regard to gardens,' says Brother Grant, 'I have seen good gardens on this earth, but I never saw any to compare with those that were there. I saw flowers of numerous kinds, and some with fifty to a hundred different colored flowers growing upon one stalk'" (*Journal of Discourses*, 4:135–36).

IS IT DIFFERENT IN THE SPIRIT WORLD FOR THE RIGHTEOUS AND THE WICKED?

In the Book of Mormon, the prophet Alma wrote: "Now, concerning the state of the soul between death and the resurrection . . . the spirits of those who are righteous are received into a state of happiness, which is called paradise, a state of rest, a state of peace, where they shall rest from all their troubles and from all care, and sorrow.

"And then shall it come to pass, that the spirits of the wicked, yea, who are evil—for behold, they have no part nor portion of the Spirit of the Lord; for behold, they chose evil works rather than good; . . . there shall be weeping, and wailing, and gnashing of teeth, and this because of their own iniquity, being led captive by the will of the devil.

"Now this is the state of the souls of the wicked, yea, in darkness, and a state of awful, fearful looking for the fiery indignation of the wrath of God upon them; thus they remain in this state, as well as the righteous in paradise, until the time of their resurrection" (Alma 40:11–14).

When the righteous die they enter a state or condition referred to as paradise. It is a state of rest and waiting where they are free from the pains and sorrows of this world. But not all people will immediately experience this state of rest in paradise. The wicked enter a condition called spirit prison or "hell" where they suffer spiritual torment as a consequence of the sins they have not repented of while on earth. It seems more accurate to consider these two states as *conditions* rather than *places*. The prophets have taught that the wicked and the righteous (since the time of Christ's visit to the spirit world while his body was in the tomb) go to the same place at death.

President Brigham Young explained it this way: "The Prophet lays down his body, he lays down his life, and his spirit goes to the world of spirits; the persecutor of the Prophet dies, and he goes to Hades; they both go to one place, and they are not to be separated yet. Now understand, that this is part of the great sermon the Lord is preaching in his providence, the righteous and the wicked are together in Hades" (*Discourses of Brigham Young*, 377).

Remember, the spirit world is like this world. It is actually an extension of this world. Just as the righteous and the unrighteous live in the same cities, walk on the same streets, shop in the same stores, and are not physically separated in this world, the same is true in the spirit world. Just as the righteous tend to meet and congregate together in this sphere, the righteous spirits in the spirit world tend to congregate there also. And just as one person could be living in a state of happiness (paradise) in his house here in mortality, another person in the same city could be living in a condition of "hell" as a result of the consequences of immorality, drug abuse, or alcoholism.

WHAT DO PEOPLE DO IN THE SPIRIT WORLD?

In an article entitled, "The Spirit World, Our Next Home," printed in the January, 1977, *Ensign*, Dale Mouritsen explained: "Apparently, righteous people in the spirit world are organized just as they are here, arranged in families and quorums. Priesthood operates there as it operates here." President Brigham Young declared: "When the faithful Elders, holding this Priesthood, go into the spirit world they carry with them the same power and Priesthood that they had while in the mortal tabernacle"

(*Discourses of Brigham Young,* 132; see also D&C 124:130). The blessings of the priesthood are thus present in the spirit world. One elder who passed beyond the veil and returned spoke of the order he saw there:

"While I was in the spirit world I observed that the people there were busy, and that they were perfectly organized for the work they were doing. It seemed to me a continuation of the work we are doing here,—something like going from one stake to another. There was nothing there that seemed particularly strange to me, everything being natural" (Peter E. Johnson, *Relief Society Magazine,* Aug. 1920, 455).

IS THE SPIRIT WORLD EXACTLY LIKE THIS ONE OR ARE THERE SOME DIFFERENCES THERE?

Apparently some things are quite different. In this world we are very conditioned to view things in a past, present, or future setting. Time is different there. Brigham Young described it in these words:

"The brightness and glory of the next apartment is inexpressible. It is not encumbered so that when we advance in years we have to be stubbing along and be careful lest we fall down. . . . But yonder, how different! They move with ease and like lightning. . . . If we want to behold Jerusalem as it was in the days of the Savior; or if we want to see the Garden of Eden as it was when created, there we are, and we see it as it existed spiritually, for it was created first spiritually and then temporally, and spiritually it still remains. And when there we may behold the earth as at the dawn of creation, or we may visit any city we please that exists upon its surface" (*Discourses of Brigham Young,* 380).

HOW LONG DOES A PERSON STAY IN THE SPIRIT WORLD?

The answer to this question depends on certain things, such as when you lived, how righteous you were, and if you have sins of which you have not repented. The spirit world basically is a place of waiting for resurrection. Since different people are resurrected at different times, the amount of time one waits in the spirit world varies. There is a definite order to the resurrection (see D&C 88:97–102). A person is resurrected when his or her spirit is reunited with his body. Generally speaking, the resurrection from death begins with the very best, Jesus Christ, and ends with the very worst, the sons of perdition. There are two parts of the resurrection: the first resurrection—also called the resurrection of life—and the last resurrection—also called the resurrection of damnation (see John 5:29). The first resurrection serves two categories of people: the "morning" of the first resurrection (for those raised to a celestial inheritance) and the "afternoon" of the first resurrection (which will provide a terrestrial inheritance for those so qualified). The last resurrection will serve two categories of people: those who have lived telestial lives and those who have become sons of perdition.

The order of the resurrection involves not only the four categories of people just mentioned but designates also different times when they come forth from their graves.

The Apostle Paul reminds us that Christ was the first to be resurrected (see 1 Corinthians 15:20), and the Doctrine and Covenants further teaches that certain righteous people who lived from the time of Adam down to the time of Christ were "with Christ in his resurrection" (D&C 133:54–55; see also Alma 40:18–19). The resurrection of these people took place during what is called the morning of the first resurrection. This resurrection will continue when Christ comes in his glory at the time of his second coming. Those resurrected at that time will be said to have also come forth in the morning of the first resurrection.

During this same time the telestial people of the earth will be burned by the brightness of the coming of Christ (see D&C 5:19). Following the burning of the wicked and the resurrection of the celestial people, the terrestrial people who have died will then be resurrected. This will happen during what is called the afternoon of the first resurrection. Having died, the telestial people and sons of perdition will remain in the spirit world during the 1,000 years of the Millennium. At the end of the Millennium, these souls will finally come forth from the graves as part of the last resurrection.

WHAT WILL OUR BODIES BE LIKE WHEN WE ARE RESURRECTED?

We will be resurrected with tangible bodies of flesh and bone (not blood), quickened by the spirit, just as Jesus was (see Luke 24:36–39). Our resurrected body will resemble our mortal body, but will be an immortal, perfected body (see Alma 11:45, 40:23). Some people mistakenly believe that we will be resurrected with only spirit bodies. This belief results from an incorrect interpretation of Paul's letter to the Corinthians where he states, "flesh and blood cannot inherit the kingdom of God" (1 Corinthians 15:50).

Joseph Smith helped clarify Paul's writing when he stated, "God Almighty Himself dwells in eternal fire; flesh and blood cannot go there, for all corruption is devoured by the fire. . . . When our flesh is quickened by the Spirit, there will be no blood in this tabernacle" (*Teachings of the Prophet Joseph Smith,* 367). On another occasion Joseph taught, "Flesh and blood cannot go there; but flesh and bones, quickened by the Spirit of God, can" (*Teachings of the Prophet Joseph Smith,* 326).

Once we are raised from the dead, our bodies will be either celestial, terrestrial, or telestial in nature (see 1 Corinthians 15:39–42; D&C 88:27–31), depending on the type of life we have chosen to live.

So when we appear at the "final judgment" there will be no surprise as to which kingdom we will inherit since we will already be resurrected with one of the three types of bodies. In essence we will "wear our judgment to court."

Resurrection is a priesthood ordinance. Just as a person must be baptized and then be ordained with authority in order to baptize others, so also must a person be resurrected and then ordained by one holding the proper priesthood keys to be able to perform this ordinance (see President Spencer W. Kimball, *Ensign,* May 1977, 49). What a blessing it will be to worthy priesthood holders to perform this ordinance for deceased loved ones of their families.

To summarize then, the third act of this eternal play has two parts, the spirit world and the resurrection. How we live in Act II and the choices we make here will determine where we'll be and what we'll be doing in Act III. For the wicked there awaits sorrow, punishment, and remorse in the spirit world and a resurrection to a telestial order. For the righteous, the spirit world will be a place of rest and peace awaiting a glorious resurrection. Ours is the freedom to choose.

Todd Parker was born in Ogden, Utah. He set a state pole vault record in high school and won the Scholar Athlete award at Weber State, where he obtained his bachelor's degree. He also holds M.Ed. and Ed.D. degrees from BYU. He taught seminary for fourteen years and institute for five. He has also taught at EFY every year since it began in 1976. He currently serves on the BYU 13th Stake high council.

5

LEARNING TO RECEIVE AND RECOGNIZE THE PROMPTINGS OF THE SPIRIT

Ronald Bartholomew

While I was serving a mission in Pusan, South Korea, I had an experience that taught me the importance of receiving and recognizing messages from the Lord. I was contacting a referral for the first time. My companion and I greeted the woman of the house and introduced ourselves as "elders of The Church of Jesus Christ of Latter-day Saints." Several other women were in the home. She turned to them and said, "The elders from the Church have come to visit!" Much to our surprise, they all burst into laughter. "How could you be an elder?" she exclaimed. "You don't look a day over fifteen!" We had to work with these people for several weeks before they came to receive and recognize us as true messengers sent to them from the Lord. We were finally able to see this woman, her family, and many of her friends join our tiny branch.

One of the greatest gifts our Father in Heaven has given

us is the promise of the constant companionship of the Holy Ghost. But, just as with these Korean Saints, there may be times when we are either not ready to receive his promptings, or don't recognize them when they come. Learning to receive and recognize the promptings of the Spirit is an exciting and challenging task that goes on throughout our entire lives. Elder S. Dilworth Young of the First Council of the Seventy taught: "I can testify to you that there will be none of you [that will] have any adventure greater, more thrilling, and more joyful than finding out how to interpret the Spirit which comes into you bearing testimony of the truth. Young folks have to learn how, so do we older folks. We have to find out the technique by which the Spirit whispers in our hearts. We have to learn to hear it and to understand it and to know when we have it, and that sometimes takes a long time" (in Conference Report, April 1959, 59).

I believe we can do this, and likewise have joy in the journey. But it requires two things on our part. First, we must pay the personal price required to be ready and worthy to receive promptings from the Holy Ghost. Secondly, we must be able to recognize the impressions of the Holy Ghost once we receive them.

BEING READY AND WORTHY TO RECEIVE THE HOLY GHOST

William Faulkner's book entitled *Go Down Moses* tells the story of a young man named Jim who was on a quest for something he very much wanted to experience. Each year he would go hunting with the men and boys of his rural community, hoping each time to catch a glimpse of a bear they all called "Old Ben." The bear had become a "legend" of sorts—for years he had raided the farmers' feeding troughs and carried away pigs, calves, and other livestock. Although he had been shot at point-blank range, caught in traps, and pursued by dogs—he could not be killed. He was immortal—or so they believed. They could always distinguish his tracks by his front left paw, which had once been caught and mangled in a trap in an unsuccessful attempt to capture the elusive animal.

While the men spent much of their time hanging around camp, talking about old times, the boys would often go squirrel hunting. But Jim was different. He was compelled to hunt down Old Ben, and he left camp early each morning with his rifle and compass, in search of the ghostly bear. He took his rifle mainly for self-defense, for he didn't want to kill Old Ben. He only wanted to get close enough to see him. However, after several days of tracking, he became discouraged.

One day, Jim's father surprised him by asking, "Have you seen Old Ben yet?"

A little embarrassed, the young man sheepishly admitted, "No."

"Have you seen any fresh prints?"

"No."

"Well," his father continued, "It's because you ain't looked right yet."

"Well, then, how?" the boy blurted out.

His father said, "Well, likely he's been watching you. . . . He's smart. That's how he's lived so long. It's the gun. Old Ben knows what a gun is. You will have to choose between seeing Old Ben and carrying your gun for defense."

The boy decided his father was right, and, after a sleepless night, Jim left camp the next morning with only a compass and an old silver watch his father had given him. After searching for more than nine hours and never even seeing the bear's tracks, he was completely discouraged. He had already voluntarily given up his gun, but standing alone in the woods, he wondered what else he could do. Suddenly it became clear to him. He hadn't given up enough; something more was required. Old Ben was watching him—he was sure of that, and he sensed that the watch and compass might be keeping the bear at a distance. He would have to give up everything if he wanted to see this bear! So, hesitantly, he hung his watch and compass on a tree and entered the forest—alone.

It wasn't long before he came to the horrifying realization that he was lost. He tried desperately to find his way back to the tree where his watch and compass hung—but it was all in vain. Discouraged, he sat down on a log in the middle of a swampy meadow. As he sat there, he was shocked to see the unmistakable, distinctive paw print of Old Ben in the soggy wet ground. As he stared at the print, he realized it was slowly filling up with water. "Wait," he thought, "It must be fresh!"

Slowly standing, then quietly walking, Jim followed Old Ben's tracks. Eventually, they led him to a small clearing in a wilderness grove, where suddenly he saw Old Ben emerge, standing upright on his two hind legs, waving his forepaws in the air. Then to his surprise, the bear fell to all fours and moved across the clearing toward a tree. Jim's eye caught the last ray of glinting sunlight as it reflected off of his compass and the watch, which hung there. The bear looked over its shoulder, directly at Jim, and then disappeared into the woods.

We might compare this young man's struggle to catch a glimpse of Old Ben to the effort we must make to be worthy to receive the companionship of the Holy Ghost. First, the boy had to search hard, over an extended period of time to find "the bear." We have to do the same. Joseph Smith found the scripture that answered his question and opened the door for the restoration of the gospel in the book of James (Holy Bible, page 1538), not on the first page of the Bible in the book of Genesis. Likewise, Enos had to pray all day and all night before the Lord spoke peace to his soul. Alma the Younger had a similar experience: "I testify unto you that I do know that these things whereof I have spoken are true. And how do ye suppose that I know of their surety? Behold, I say unto you they are made known unto me by the Holy Spirit of God. Behold, I have fasted and prayed many days that I might know these things of myself. And now I do know of myself that they are true; for the Lord God hath made them manifest unto me by his Holy Spirit" (Alma 5:45–46).

If we want to have the Spirit in our lives, we also must search the scriptures, ponder, pray, and even fast on a regular, consistent basis, over time. But, oh, what joy we can have in this journey, as we prepare ourselves to receive the promptings of the Holy Ghost!

Secondly, the young man laid down those things that were getting in the way of his "seeing the bear." Do we have things in our lives that are preventing us from having the constant companionship of the Holy Ghost? Our sins will prevent us from enjoying the Spirit. As a member of the Godhead, the Holy Ghost will only dwell in "holy temples." Do you remember the story of King Lamoni's father, who had once rejected Ammon and his brothers? Later he received them because of their unqualified love for his son. After Aaron taught him the basic gospel principles, the old king exclaimed, "O God, Aaron hath told me that there is a God; and if there is a God, and if thou art God, wilt thou make thyself known unto me, and I will give away all my sins to know thee" (Alma 22:18). The king's willingness to purge himself of all his sins was answered by the Lord with an outpouring of the Holy Ghost so strong that he fell to the earth, physically overwhelmed. Once you and I show our willingness to give up all that is between us and God, we will also be worthy to receive the Holy Ghost.

RECOGNIZING THE PROMPTINGS OF THE HOLY GHOST

Part of the challenge of learning to recognize communication from the Holy Ghost is that his messages often come to us in ways that might be different from what we are expecting. One day the students in my seminary class were discussing the different ways the Holy Ghost can manifest himself to us. Right in the middle of the discussion, a young woman blurted out, "I have felt the Spirit!" Everyone turned and looked at her, and she excitedly explained: "All my life as I've read or heard others explain their experiences with the Holy Ghost, I've thought I must be spiritually deaf or something because I've never had those kinds of experiences." As we studied some of the scriptures in the Doctrine and Covenants that explain how the Holy Ghost can speak to us, she was able to relate to some of them personally. The scriptures teach that we can receive communication from the Holy Ghost in a variety of ways. For example, D&C 8:2 says, "I will tell you in your mind and in your heart, by the Holy Ghost." Sometimes the Holy Ghost speaks to our mind, and other times we feel his messages in our heart.

In the fall of 1842 Joseph Smith wrote two letters to the Saints in Nauvoo concerning baptisms for the dead. He begins his second letter (Section 128:1) by explaining the reason he is writing about baptisms for the dead. It was because "that subject seems to occupy my mind, and press itself upon my feelings the strongest."

That is how the Spirit works—it presses itself upon our feelings or occupies our minds. Have you ever felt strongly that you should pursue a particular course, or that you should not do a particular thing? That can be the Holy Ghost. Or have you ever had a particular thought "occupy your mind" until you acted upon it? That can be the Holy Ghost, too. Sometimes the difficult thing is discerning if it is the Spirit that is prompting you to do or not to do a particular thing, or if the message is coming from somewhere else. However, D&C 11:12 says "put your trust in that Spirit which leadeth to do good—yea, to do justly, to walk humbly, to judge righteously; and this is my Spirit."

Have you ever experienced a feeling of peace concerning a particular matter or decision? That is another way the Holy Ghost can communicate with us. When Oliver Cowdery was wondering about the truthfulness of the work he was about to engage in as Joseph Smith's scribe, the Lord taught him this: "If you desire a further witness, cast your mind upon the night that you cried unto me in your heart, that you might know concerning the truth of these things. Did I not speak peace to your mind concerning the matter? . . . And now, behold, you have received a witness" (D&C 6:22–24).

Yet another way that the Holy Ghost can speak to us is described in D&C 9:8–9. The Lord says:

" . . . if it is right I will cause that your bosom shall burn within you; therefore, you shall feel that it is right. But if it be not right you shall have no such feelings, but you shall have a stupor of thought."

Whether it be a peaceful feeling that sets you at ease, an urging to do or not to do a certain thing, or a feeling of warmth that fills your heart and soul and bears witness to a truth, these are all ways the Lord communicates "in your mind and in your heart, by the Holy Ghost" (D&C 8:2). We need to be careful, however, that the spectacular images and stories of others or even the scriptures do not distract us from enjoying the most common form of heavenly communication, the still small voice.

President Spencer W. Kimball proclaimed: "The burning bushes, the smoking mountains, the Cumorahs, and the Kirtlands were realities, but they were the exceptions. The great volume of revelation came to Moses and Joseph and comes to today's prophet in the less-spectacular way—that of deep impressions but without the spectacle or glamour of dramatic events. Always expecting the spectacular, many will miss entirely the constant flow of revealed communication" (*Church News,* January 5, 1974).

STOP, LOOK, AND LISTEN

You can experience these communications from the Holy Ghost on a regular basis, if you are doing your best to live right and if you are really listening for them. However, it is possible to be too distracted or preoccupied to heed a spiritual prompting. In the Book of Mormon there is an example of the Nephites doing this. They actually heard the voice of Heavenly Father three times before they recognized who it was and what he was saying: "And again the third time they did hear the voice, and did open their ears to hear it; and their eyes were towards the sound thereof; and they did look steadfastly towards heaven, from whence the sound came. And behold, the third time they did understand the voice which they heard" (3 Nephi 11:5–6).

What was different about the third time they heard the sound, that they were finally able to comprehend the message? I remember what I learned in kindergarten about crossing the street: STOP, LOOK, and LISTEN! Think about this in relation to the Nephites' experience in hearing the voice of the Lord: they STOPPED, they LOOKED, and they LISTENED. We, too, must stop in our busy lives, look "towards the sound thereof," and listen intently to receive his messages.

President David O. McKay related the following story, which emphasizes the importance of making ourselves available to the promptings that might come.

"One day in Salt Lake City a son kissed his mother good morning, took his dinner bucket, and went to City Creek Canyon where he worked. He was a switchman on the train that was carrying logs out of the canyon. Before noon his body was brought back lifeless. The mother was inconsolable. She could not be reconciled to that tragedy—her boy just in his early twenties so suddenly taken away. The funeral was held, and words of consolation were spoken, but she was not consoled. She couldn't understand it.

"One forenoon, so she says, after her husband had gone to his office to attend to his duties as a member of the Presiding Bishopric, she lay in a relaxed state on the bed, still yearning and praying for some consolation. She said that her son appeared and said, 'Mother, you needn't worry. That was merely an accident. I gave the signal to the engineer to move on, and as the train started, I jumped for the handle of the freight car, and my foot got caught in a sagebrush, and I fell under the wheel. I went to Father soon after that, but he was so busy in the office I couldn't influence him—I couldn't make any impression upon him, and I tried again. Today I come to you to give you that comfort and tell you that I am happy'" (*Gospel Ideals* [1953], 525–26).

If it is possible to be so engrossed, even in good things,

that we are unable to "hear" or receive an impression like this one, we must try harder and work to be constantly receptive to the promptings of the Spirit. In Revelation 3:20, the Lord reminds us: "Behold, I stand at the door, and knock: if any man hear my voice and open the door, I will come in to him, and will sup with him, and he with me." My brothers, my sisters, and my friends, may you and I always be in a position to recognize and receive the promptings of the Holy Ghost.

Ron Bartholomew was born in Lehi, Utah, and is the oldest of seven children. After serving a mission in Pusan, Korea, he received both bachelor's and master's degrees from BYU. He met his wife, Kristen, when they were both working at the MTC, and after one year of dating they were married in the Provo Temple. He is currently teaching seminary at Orem High School and classes at the institute of religion at Utah Valley State College. He and his wife have five children. Ron enjoys woodworking, gardening, computers, and camping, but his very favorite thing in the whole world is gummi bears.

6

"ON BELAY":
THE POWER OF
COVENANTS

Scott Simmons

Climbing," I yelled.

"On belay," my friend hollered back.

With that assurance I began my ascent. Slowly and carefully I began to climb the rock wall before me. This was my first time rock climbing, and despite my nervousness, I was confident. The source of my confidence was simple, my friend was "on belay." That term may be new to you as it was to me just a few years before this experience, so let me explain.

I first learned what "on belay" meant on a trip my friend Todd Murdock and I took to St. George, Utah. We had gone down for the weekend to hike the Narrows in Zion Canyon and to spend some time with Todd's family. Hiking and spending time with Todd's family was fun; however, the best part of the trip came on our way home. Driving out of St. George we noticed a group of people rappelling off the Sugar Loaf, a popular spot for that sport. Todd and I decided to stop and watch for a while.

It was incredible to see. There were two groups of rappellers descending two separate areas. The first group was

coming down a flat wall, while the second group was working its way off a section of the cliff that resembled a human
nose. This "nose" was about twenty feet long and lay at
about a forty-five degree angle. Then the rock cut back into
the face. That meant that for the rest of the drop to the
ground the rappellers couldn't touch the wall; they had to
free-fall for about one hundred and fifty feet. As we watched,
the young men in this group would rappel down the nose,
then jump out into thin air, slide down the rope, and land
perfectly on the ground without so much as messing up
their hair. We found out later that they were professionals.

As I said, it was incredible to see how skillful and daring
they were. Todd and I watched for some time, and I began
to think it would be awesome to try rappelling. Just as I
had that thought, some of the rappellers from the second
group hollered down at us. At first we thought they must
be talking to someone else. However, when I looked
around, there was no one else nearby. So I gestured as if to
ask, "Are you talking to us?"

They responded, "Yeah, you guys. Do you want to do
this?"

I couldn't believe they were actually asking if we wanted
to rappel. I was stunned. I remember thinking, *Yes, I want
to do this* and then in the next instant thinking, *Do I want
to do this?* However, before I could talk myself out of it,
Todd and I had quickly made our way to the top of the
"Loaf." Before we could give it a second thought we had
introduced ourselves, thanked our new friends for inviting
us to join them, and started our first rappelling lesson.

After a few minutes of instruction, our friends asked if
we were ready to try. Hesitantly, I agreed to go first. I think
my new friend sensed my fear and so to assure me he said,
"Don't worry, I will be on belay."

I had learned from our lesson that "on belay" meant
that he would be at the bottom with the end of the rope
secured to him. This meant two things: First, having the
rope secured to him meant that the rope would be steady
as I made my descent. Second, if something went wrong

and I could not stop my fall, he could. This gave me some comfort; however, because I had never rappelled before, I was still nervous and concerned.

While my friend made his way down to be on belay, the other rappellers helped me get into gear and get the feel of the rope. When everything was ready I hollered, "Rappelling."

My new friend yelled back, "On belay." And with that, I started my descent. I was really cruising. I remember thinking, *This isn't so hard. In fact, this is a piece of cake.* Just then one of the rappellers reminded me that I was supposed to go over the edge. With a lot more fear and a lot less confidence, I looked down. As I did my friend on belay yelled, "Just lean back and trust the rope."

I remember thinking, *Okay, no problem. It's only two hundred feet down, and my new friend won't let me fall.* Just kidding. What I actually thought was, *Right! It's two hundred feet down, I have never done this before, and I hardly know you. What if this is some kind of rappellers' joke? They find some poor curious fool, lure him in, and then watch him become a greasy spot on the ground below.*

The fact is, I was scared to death. Yet, I knew I had to do this. So, I began my slow descent to the end of the nose. Because I didn't yet trust the rope, I clung to the rock face and slid down rather than rappelling. My friend kept yelling, "Lean back and trust the rope." I tried to, but my fear kept me clinging to the face. Finally, the moment of truth arrived; I reached the tip of the nose. From here on down it was a free fall. I would no longer be able to cling to the face for security. I would have to trust my friend and the rope. With a silent prayer and mustering all the courage I could, I held my breath and leaned out. At first I thought I was dead because my heart had stopped beating. I slowly opened one eye and then the other and found I was still alive—more alive than I think I had ever been—suspended in midair, dangling one hundred and fifty feet above the ground. The feeling was exhilarating to say the least. My new friend yelled, "See? I told you. Trust the rope."

In total control and with a newfound confidence, I slowly continued my descent. When I got about halfway down, my friend below yelled for me to stop. Mechanically I obeyed. He then asked, "Would you like to see what someone on belay can do for you?"

Curious, I replied, "Sure."

His next words hit me in the pit of my stomach. I knew it was the pit of my stomach because my heart had been there only moments before. He said simply and matter-of-factly, "Let go."

Let go! I thought. *Who is he trying to kid? It has taken every ounce of courage I could muster to go off the face, and now he's asking me to let go of the rope, leaving it connected to me only through my harness.* Letting go would mean relying totally on my friend to control my descent. You see, when rappelling, your hands perform two functions. Your lead hand is placed on the rope, in front of your body, and keeps you steady. Your other hand is placed on the rope behind your back and controls the rate of your descent. When you pull your hand away from your back, you slide down the rope. Bringing the hand into your back slows or stops your descent. Letting go of the rope meant that I would slide down the rope out of control.

I hesitated, and my friend called out once again, "Let go." Then he added, "You trust the rope, now trust me."

Reluctantly, I let go with my lead hand but still kept my other hand tight against my back. I started to turn a little, but I didn't slide. Pleased with my progress, my friend yelled again, "Let go with your other hand also."

Minutes went by that seemed like years. To this day I am not sure how I did it, but closing my eyes and holding my breath (I stopped breathing altogether would probably be a more accurate description), I let go. When I didn't move, I opened my eyes to find myself suspended in midair. I experienced the same feeling of exhilaration I had experienced when I went off the face, but it was twice as strong this time. It was unbelievable. My friend then told me to carefully take hold of the rope again. I did and continued my descent safely to the bottom.

Now, years later, I was climbing a rock wall confidently because I knew what "on belay" meant and had confidence in it. At this point you're probably saying to yourself, "Nice story, but what does this have to do with the gospel or covenants?" Let me explain.

You and I live in a fallen world. To illustrate how fallen this world is, I often ask my students to tell me all the things they would change about this world if they could. Typical answers often include: no death, relief from pain and suffering, world peace, no crime, no hate, and no fat grams. All of these are the result of living in a fallen world.

Now, not only do you and I live in a fallen world, we are fallen ourselves. This can be illustrated in the same way by simply asking what you would change about yourself if you could. Again typical student responses include: more patience and tolerance, more kindness, more love, and more control. Almost sounds like a hymn, doesn't it? (see *Hymns,* no. 131).

Because we are fallen, you and I are cut off from our Father in Heaven, both temporally and spiritually (see Alma 42:7). At the same time, we know that we are children of God, with the potential to be like him. This is why we desire a better world and a better self. It is like knowing there is something better, but we can't get to it because we are in a deep dark hole with no way out. Sounds pretty bleak, doesn't it? So much so that some around us have simply decided that since there is no way out, why not indulge? Unfortunately for them, acceptance is not escape. Or in the words of Alma, "Wickedness never was happiness" (Alma 41:10). The only way out is up, which means we have to climb. The problem is, it is an impossible climb to make on our own. Fortunately, we have not been left alone.

Our Father in Heaven has provided a way for us to get out of this hole and back to him. However, in order for us to get out, someone had to be willing to come down into the hole and show us by example the way out. Not only show us, but provide the way as well. Our brother and Savior volunteered to do this by simply saying, "Here am I, send me"(Abraham 3:27). He came down to show us how to climb out. He also provided a rope for us to use in our climb, and he is "on belay."

What does all this have to do with covenants? First, let's define covenant. Your Bible Dictionary says that a covenant is an agreement between God and man (p. 651). In the gospel covenant we agree to do certain things, and in return, God agrees to help us out of the hole and back to him. The gospel of Jesus Christ is called the new and everlasting covenant. Through living the gospel—that is, keeping our covenants—we can obtain the blessings of peace in this life and exaltation in the life to come (see D&C 59:23). In other words, the covenants that we make are the rope that binds us to the Savior and shows us the way back to our Father in Heaven. All we have to do is continue to climb the rope. If we slip, the Savior is on belay. Brother Robert J. Matthews, former dean of the religion department at BYU, said it this way: "The purpose of the gospel [the new and everlasting covenant] is to educate, perfect, and sanctify man, *lifting him to the status of a god* in celestial glory . . . . Divine covenants *mark the path* of duty and commit us to walk in it. They more fully distinguish the way of the Lord from the way of the world . . . [and] *every gospel covenant ties the individual closer to the Lord"* (*Ensign,* December 1980, 35; emphasis added).

To illustrate this, consider two of the covenants in the gospel you are probably most familiar with—baptism and the sacrament. At baptism we make a covenant with God, which we renew each week as we partake of the sacrament. As our part of the covenant we agree to: 1) be willing to take upon us the name of the Savior; 2) always remember the Savior and his sacrifice for us; and 3) keep his commandments. Doing these things ties us to the Savior and shows us the way home. Let's take a closer look at each one.

WILLING TO TAKE UPON US
THE NAME OF THE SAVIOR

What does it mean to be willing to take upon us the name of the Savior? President David O. McKay explained that being willing to take upon us the name of the Savior means that "we choose him as our leader and our ideal; and [acknowledge] he is the one perfect character in all the world" (*Gospel Ideals* [1954], 146). In other words, we declare our willingness to be called a Christian or a Latter-day Saint. This means you don't mind, in fact you are grateful, that your peers think you are a "goody-goody." It also means you are willing to do all that the Savior would ask you to do.

ALWAYS REMEMBER HIM

How do we always remember the Savior and his sacrifice for us? The ordinance of the sacrament itself is designed to help us remember (see Elder Jeffery R. Holland, *Ensign,* November 1995, 67–69). The bread reminds us of his body, which was, as one hymn describes it, "bruised, broken, torn for us" (see *Hymns,* no. 181). The water is to remind us of the blood that was shed in Gethsemane and on the cross for our sins. So the first place we can begin remembering him is during the sacrament service itself. Here are some suggestions that might help you become more aware: reread the words of the sacrament hymn; read a favorite passage of scripture on the Atonement; review your week, paying special attention to the divine help you received or offering a prayer of thanks. These are just a few ideas. For others you can ask your parents, friends, and leaders what they do.

Now, that covers the time in sacrament meeting, but what about the rest of the week? How do you remember the Savior during the week? Daily prayer and scripture reading are the best ways. Other ideas are: hanging a picture of the Savior in your room or locker at school where you will see it often, putting up "Mormonads," memorizing the words to a favorite sacrament hymn, putting inspirational stickers on your folders, doing little acts of service, being aware of the Christlike acts performed by others, or picturing the Savior going everywhere with you. These are just some suggestions. It really doesn't matter what you do to remember the Savior, the important thing is that you remember.

KEEP THE COMMANDMENTS

This can sometimes be the easiest to understand and the hardest to do. One of the reasons that we may have a hard time keeping the commandments is we don't have the right motivation. There are lots of reasons that people keep the commandments. Some do it out of fear. They don't want to have anything bad happen to them. Others keep the commandments because they know that they will get blessings. Although these reasons will work some of the time, they will not help us keep the commandments all the time. The Savior explained the one motive that will help us have a desire to keep the commandments all the time when he said, "If ye love me, keep my commandments" (John 14:15). If we truly love him, we will not want to disappoint him, we will desire to make him happy, and we will be delighted to do as he has asked us to do. That is why the love we have for our Savior is the best motive for keeping the commandments. Being willing to take his name upon us and always remembering him will help us have this motive.

That's our part of the covenant. By doing these things we bind ourselves to the Savior. We are attached to the rope. However, remember that a covenant is a two-way agreement. What is the promise if we use the rope? Not only do we have the rope to guide us and the Savior on belay, but we are promised that the Spirit will always be with us. We will have a faithful climbing companion. He will be there to warn of danger, to guide, to give light, to comfort and cleanse.

Wow, is that awesome or what? With all that help, you

can't fail. All you have to do is take hold of the rope and climb, following your partner. Or in other words, keep your covenants and follow the Spirit. Now you might be saying, "If it is that easy, why doesn't everyone do it?" I believe that one reason is many don't understand the power of covenants. The purpose of this chapter has been to help you better understand that power. Another reason why everyone doesn't keep their covenants is the temptations that surround us, inviting us to pay attention to other things rather than attending to our task.

For example, as you climb, you might be tempted to leave the rope and climb on your own. Most people do this because they think they see an easier way. These are the people Lehi saw in the great and spacious building (see 1 Nephi 8:26–27). Don't be fooled. Don't confuse "a way" or "my way" with "The Way." Those who leave the rope will fall and the fall will be great (see 1 Nephi 11:36). Those who stay connected to the rope may slip, but they will be okay because the Savior is on belay, and they are bound to him.

To conclude I want you to know that I know there is a way out of the Fall. The Savior has made possible and provided the way. He is on belay. It is up to us to take hold of the rope and start climbing. As you willingly keep your covenants you will be secure as you make your climb carefully and confidently back to the waiting arms of a loving Father in Heaven.

"Climbing!"

"On belay!"

Scott Simmons served a mission to Cleveland, Ohio, then attended BYU and worked at the MTC. He is currently a part-time instructor in the Department of Church History at BYU. He loves teaching the gospel, outdoor adventures, and kissing his wife. He and his wife, Nancy, live in American Fork, Utah.

7

THE BEST THREE HOURS OF THE WEEK

John Bytheway

Last year at *Especially for Youth,* I asked the youth in one of my classes what would have to change so that they could get more from their Sunday meetings. Hands went up. The first young man I called on said, "It's too early."

"Oh, really, what time do your meetings start?"

"Eleven," he said as the class snickered. I wrote, "too early" on the board as I mumbled to myself, "That's impressive."

"What else?" I asked.

"Boring speakers," was the second response. *I kind of expected that one,* I thought as I wrote on the board.

"There's too many noisy kids during the meeting," someone else said, so I wrote "bawling babies" on the board.

"Okay," I continued, "What else could we change?"

"Our teacher thinks he's funny, and he's not." I wrote, "teacher not funny" on the board and wondered why this wasn't going the way I planned. Finally, a young woman changed everything when she said, "Maybe we could change our attitude."

"Yeah!" I said as I glared at the class and wrote

"attitude" on the board without looking. "Perhaps we could change our attitude!"

You see, for years, I've been noticing something every Sunday which makes me feel a little frustrated and uncomfortable. You know what it is? I'll tell you: *Bored teenagers at church.* There's no reason for it. The gospel is the single most exciting thing on this earth, and we ought to be the most interested and energetic people in the world because we have it. Would you like to get more out of your church meetings? Nod up and down, please. Thank you. Well, good, because we're going to look at six things you can do to get more from the best three hours of the week we often call "church." Let's spell the word "church," a letter at a time, and learn something from each letter.

C IS FOR CHOOSE

Recently I read a story about a restaurant manager who was always in a good mood. One of his friends asked him how he always managed to stay so happy. He replied, "Each morning I wake up and say to myself, 'You have two choices today. You can choose to be in a good mood or you can choose to be in a bad mood.' I choose to be in a good mood. Each time something bad happens, I can choose to be a victim or I can choose to learn from it. I choose to learn from it. Every time someone comes to me complaining, I can choose to accept their complaining or I can point out the positive side of life. I choose the positive side of life."

Several years later, this man was held up at gunpoint and shot. How did he react to that situation? I mean, being in a good mood in the morning is one thing—but what kind of mood are you in after you've been shot? He continued: "As I lay on the floor, I remembered that I had two choices: I could choose to live, or I could choose to die. I chose to live. . . . When they wheeled me into the emergency room and I saw the expressions on the faces of the doctors and nurses, I got really scared. In their eyes, I read, 'He's a dead man.' I knew I needed to take action. . . ."

There was a big burly nurse shouting questions at me. She asked if I was allergic to anything. 'Yes,' I replied. The doctors and nurses stopped working as they waited for my reply. I took a deep breath and yelled, 'Bullets!' Over their laughter, I told them, 'I am choosing to live. Operate on me as if I am alive, not dead'" (*Chicken Soup for the Soul at Work* [1996], 211–13).

Needless to say, he lived. Can you imagine the doctors' and nurses' reaction to this man? The guy is bleeding to death, and he chooses to show a sense of humor! Now to the point—If a man who is bleeding to death can choose to have a sense of humor, do you suppose the teenager reading this book could choose to enjoy his or her church meetings? You bet. It all comes down to as simple a thing as saying to yourself, "I'm going to get something out of my meetings today." But the choice doesn't begin on Sunday morning. It begins on Saturday night. President Ezra Taft Benson once said, "It seems to me the following should be avoided on the Sabbath: Overworking and staying up late Saturday so that you are exhausted the next day" (*Ensign,* May 1971, 6). I think the danger with most teenagers is not overworking, but overplaying. Wouldn't it be wonderful to hear a teenager say on a Saturday night, "Sure, I can hang out with you guys tonight, but I can't stay out too late, because *I want to be awake for church.*" Perhaps an ordinary teen might say, "Oh, sure!" at that suggestion, but you, my friend, are not ordinary. Besides, remember when you nodded your head a few paragraphs back about wanting to get more out of church? I saw that. Keep reading.

What else can you do to get more from your meetings? Answer: take a jug with you to church. Elder Bruce R. McConkie taught, "We come into these congregations, and sometimes a speaker brings a jug of living water that has in it many gallons. And when he pours it out on the congregation, all the members have brought is a single cup and so that's all they take away. Or maybe they have their hands over the cups, and they don't get anything to

speak of" ("The Seven Deadly Heresies," *Classic Speeches,*
[Brigham Young University, Provo, Utah, 1994], 180). With
your jug in hand, you are ready to catch any living
water that comes from the pulpit. Say to yourself, "I'm
gonna learn ten new things in this talk that I didn't know
when I came in" and then keep score and see if you can
do it.

"But, Brother Bytheway," you ask, "what if the speaker
is boring?" Sorry. No promises. I'm not saying there aren't
boring speakers now and then, but have you ever noticed
that two people can come out of the same sacrament service with totally different feelings about the meeting?
Elder Henry B. Eyring told of a time when he attended
church with his father and listened to what for young
Henry had been a "dull talk." As they walked home, he
was trying to think of a way to ask his father why he had
been "beaming" during the boring meeting.

"I finally got up enough courage to ask him what he
thought of the meeting. He said it was wonderful. . . . Like
all good fathers, he must have read my mind, because he
started to laugh. He said: 'Hal, let me tell you something.
Since I was a very young man, I have taught myself to do
something in a church meeting. When the speaker begins,
I listen carefully and ask myself what it is he is trying to
say. Then, once I think I know what he is trying to accomplish, I give myself a sermon on that subject.' He let that
sink in for a moment as we walked along. Then, with that
special self-deprecating chuckle of his, he said, 'Hal, since
then I have never been to a bad meeting'" (*To Draw Closer
to God* [Deseret Book: Salt Lake City, 1997], 23).

Once again, C is for Choose. If you can change your
attitude, you've automatically changed everything else!
This Sunday, choose to get something from your meetings!
Let's move on.

H IS FOR HOLY SABBATH

If you saw the October 1997 *New Era,* you probably read
the article about Eli Herring. If you don't recognize the

name, well, there's a reason for that. You see, Eli made a certain choice after graduating from BYU. *USA Today* said he would have been a first-round draft pick in the NFL, but he decided not to enter the draft. The reason? He didn't want to play football on Sunday. When the press interviewed his father, Eli's father said, "Our great-grand-fathers called it the Holy Sabbath. Our grandfathers called it the Sabbath. Our fathers called it Sunday. And we call it the weekend" (David L. Herring, *Cougar Club Newsletter,* May 9, 1995, Vol. 10, No. 9). If we're not careful, we might follow in the footsteps of the world and allow the Sabbath to be become less and less important in our lives. President Gordon B. Hinckley said, "The Sabbath of the Lord is becoming the play day of the people. It is a day of golf and football on television, of buying and selling in our stores and markets. Are we moving to mainstream America as some observers believe? In this I fear we are" (*Ensign,* November 1997, 69). If someone made a secret videotape of all your activities on Sunday, would they be able to tell that, for you, this day is different from the others in the week? The scriptures tell us that how we treat the Sabbath is a sign to the Lord of how we feel about him. "And hallow my sabbaths; and they shall be a sign between me and you, that ye may know that I am the Lord your God" (Ezekiel 20:20).

Commenting on this verse, Elder Russell M. Nelson said: "If, on the one hand, my interests on the Sabbath day are turned to activities such as pro football games or worldly movies, the sign from me to him would clearly be that my devotions do not favor him. If, on the other hand, my Sabbath interests are focused on the Lord and his teachings, on the family, or on folks who are sick or poor or needy, that sign would likewise be evidence to God. I have concluded that our activities on the Sabbath will be appropriate when we honestly consider them to be our personal sign of our commitment to the Lord" ("Reflection and Resolution," *Speeches of the Year,* 1989 [1990], 130).

You can get more from your Sunday meetings by re-enthroning the Sabbath day in your life. Because Sunday television has become such a temptation for sports fans, Elder Joe J. Christensen recommended using your VCR to tape the games, then watch them on another day when you can fast-forward through the commercials. (Fast-forwarding through commercials is one of life's great joys). Sometimes it makes you wonder if the head dudes at the NFL got together and said, "How can we really irritate the Mormons? I know, let's have all the games on Sunday! Ah ha ha ha. Yeah, but let's have one special game on *Monday night!* AH HA HA HA!" Elder Joe J. Christensen also said, "Make Sundays special, and they will help make you special in the sight of the Lord. Who was it that said, 'It is not so much that the Jews kept the Sabbath,' but rather, over the centuries, 'The Sabbath kept the Jews.' Keeping the Lord's day holy will do the same for you" (*BYU Devotional and Fireside Speeches*, 1993–1994, 64). H stands for Holy Sabbath. Make that day your sign to the Lord about how you feel about him.

U IS FOR UNITY

One summer, while speaking at a youth conference, I was pulled aside by an adult leader who said, "Could you talk about gossip? We have a problem with that here." I did my best, but a young woman in the testimony meeting did it better than I. She said, "We've been studying about Zion in seminary, and it sounds to me like we're supposed to be friends." Oh, nicely said. We *are* supposed to be friends. If Satan really wants to destroy the Church, I think he'll start from the inside and work outward. The outside-in approach, used by those who publish anti-Mormon books and videos, will never do much damage. President Heber J. Grant taught:

"Our enemies have never done anything that has injured this work of God, and they never will. I look around, I read, I reflect, and I ask the question, Where are the men of influence, of power and prestige, who have worked against the Latter-day Saints? Where is the reputation, for honor and courage, of the governors of Missouri and Illinois, the judges, and all others who have come here to Utah on special missions against the Latter-day Saints? Where are there people to do them honor? They cannot be found. . . . We need have no fears, we Latter-day Saints. God will continue to sustain this work; He will sustain the right. If we are loyal, if we are true, if we are worthy of this gospel, of which God has given us a testimony, there is no danger that the world can ever injure us. We can never be injured, my brethren and sisters, by any mortals, *except ourselves*" (Heber J. Grant, *Gospel Standards*, 85; emphasis added).

The anti-Mormons will continue to do their work. Don't be alarmed or concerned. Just do your part to strengthen your own ward or stake.

May I suggest that next time you go to church, you take some paper or stationery or thank-you notes? Imagine what you could do to build unity in your ward by expressing gratitude to those who teach and serve you. Perhaps an elderly brother gives a talk in your ward, and at the end of the meeting, you hand him a note. When he goes home, he reads this message from you: "Dear Brother Jones, I am so glad I came to church today. Thank you for talking about the sacrament. I learned a lot of things I didn't know. Thank you for preparing so well. I'm glad we're in the same ward. Your friend, Jennifer." Now, how do you think Brother Jones will feel? How about you? That's the nice thing about gratitude. It makes everyone feel better. You also have Sunday School teachers and advisers. They deserve thanks too! Have we learned anything from the ten lepers in Luke 17:12–19? Remember when only one of the ten who had been healed returned to give thanks? That's only 10%! Are you one of the 10% or one of the 90%? We can do better than that. We have to! Because it sounds to me like we're supposed to be friends. U is for Unity.

R IS FOR RESPECT

As you may know, sometimes I have the chance to teach at *Especially for Youth*. I am also a Gospel Doctrine teacher for the sixteen- and seventeen-year-olds in my ward. Can I tell you something? I would much rather have you be disrespectful to me at EFY than to your teachers at church. I know from experience that it's a lot harder to teach a class week after week than to go to EFY and give a few planned and practiced talks. More importantly, I do not have a "calling" to give talks at EFY. Your teachers, on the other hand, have been called by the Lord through the bishop to teach you, and you were given an opportunity to sustain them by the uplifted hand! I have felt disrespect as a Sunday School teacher. I know that your teachers shed real tears over their students. You will be in their shoes one day. Unfortunately, some students show up to class with an "I-dare-you-to-teach-me" attitude, and then simply "endure" class while making jokes and disrupting. I firmly believe, that when you disrespect your called-and-sustained teachers, you disrespect the One who called them. In other words, you disrespect the Lord. Folks, that's a sin.

Our modern media doesn't teach respect. It teaches that you have to dish out clever put-downs to earn applause. Don't believe it. It's false. The Lord teaches reverence and respect. Sometimes we're not very good at explaining how to listen to a talk. In sacrament meeting, we often see parents taking fussy children out of the chapel. That's appropriate. Perhaps because we've seen that happen, we've assumed that we can leave anytime we want and it's okay. It isn't. In fact, it's rude. It's *very* rude to walk out on a speaker or a teacher while they're in the middle of their presentation. It's even worse to invite someone else to leave with you. As a Sunday School teacher, almost every week, I have to go out into the foyer and literally pull people off the couches into class. It shouldn't be that way. You're teenagers now, and as you've often been told, perhaps too often, you are some of the Lord's choicest spirits.

My advice? Act like it. You know where you're supposed to be. And your attendance in Sunday School shouldn't be based on whether the teacher is funny or not. We don't go to church because it's fun. We go because we love the Lord, and he wants us there to strengthen each other and to remember him. Show genuine respect to your leaders and teachers, and you'll be showing it to the Lord.

C IS FOR COVENANTS

As you know, we come to church to partake of the sacrament and in that way renew our baptismal covenant. We take the sacrament every week, and we cannot take doing so lightly. I recently came across this poem whose author is unknown to me:

> There was envy in the glances that a lovely matron cast,
> At the coiffure [hairdo] of her neighbor while the sacrament was passed,
> And a teenage girl, I noticed, though a timid lass and shy,
> Watched a youthful priest intently through the corner of her eye,
> As he sat behind the table where the water trays were spread,
> She was not remembering Jesus, nor the prayer the priest had said.
> There was nothing reverential in the things the Cub Scout drew,
> On the pages of the hymn book till the sacrament was through.
> Not a thought of Jesus' passion entered careless elders' minds,
> As they whispered to each other and the girls they sat behind.
> And the high priest's brow was furrowed while he stole a secret glance,

At a checkbook's dismal story of his failures in
  finance.
There were hundreds in the chapel, but the wor-
  shipers were few,
And I couldn't help but wonder what the Lord
  Himself would do—
Yes I couldn't help but wonder what the Lord
  Himself would say,
Should He walk into the meeting while His Saints
  behaved this way.
Would His loving eyes be saddened, would His
  countenance be grim,
While He there observed and listened to the ser-
  vice meant for Him?

I love those last three words, *meant for Him.* Somehow,
some of us think the meeting is meant for us. *Okay, everyone—teachers, speakers, advisers—your job is to devote yourselves to making me happy. If the meetings start too early or if
teachers aren't funny or if I become bored in any way, I'm leaving. I'll be napping on the couch in the foyer.* All this time,
we've been talking about "getting" more from our meetings. Now we're going to move to higher ground. We
don't go to church to "get." We go to "give." What do we
give? We give our devotion to the Savior, we give our love
and respect to our fellow ward members, we give, because
we have been given much.

President Spencer W. Kimball taught: "One good but
mistaken man I know claimed he could get more out of a
good book on Sunday than he could get in attending
church services, saying that the sermons were hardly up to
his standards. [In teenage lingo, "Our teacher thinks he's
funny and he's not."] But we do not go to Sabbath meetings to be entertained or even simply to be instructed. We
go to worship the Lord. . . . If the service is a failure to you,
you have failed" (*Faith Precedes the Miracle,* 271).

It is said that someone once asked President Kimball
what the most important word in the dictionary was. He

answered, *remember.* Why do we take the sacrament every week? Because the Lord wants us to "remember him." You'll notice that a form of the word *remember* appears twice in each of the sacrament prayers.

The next time you go to sacrament meeting, I hope you'll notice a few more things. First of all, notice how the priests tear the bread during the sacrament hymn. Why? Perhaps because Jesus' body was "bruised, broken, and torn for us." Jesus said of himself, "I am the bread of life" (John 6:35). Notice also in the words of the prayer, the bread and water are not taken to "nourish and strengthen our *bodies,*" but are blessed and sanctified "to the *souls*" of all who partake. The sacrament is more than just physical food, it's spiritual food. Also, isn't it amazing that in the most important few minutes of the best three hours of the week, the meeting is entrusted to teenage young men? President Gordon B. Hinckley said:

"When you, as a priest, kneel at the sacrament table and offer up the prayer, which came by revelation, you place the entire congregation under covenant with the Lord. Is this a small thing? It is a most important and remarkable thing.

"Now, my dear young brethren, if we are to . . . administer to the membership of the Church the emblems of the sacrifice of our Lord, then we must be worthy to do so.

"You cannot consistently so serve on the Sabbath and fail to live the standards of the Church during the week. It is totally wrong for you to take the name of the Lord in vain and indulge in filthy and unseemly talk at school or at work, and then kneel at the sacrament table on Sunday. You cannot drink beer or partake of illegal drugs and be worthy of the ministering of angels. You cannot be immoral in talk or in practice and expect the Lord to honor your service in teaching repentance or baptizing for the remission of sins. As those holding His holy priesthood, you must be worthy fellow servants" (*Ensign,* May 1988, 46).

Someone recently suggested that if Heavenly Father had

a favorite scripture, he would arrange it so that his children would hear it often. He would have the person repeating the scripture kneel down. And the message within the scripture would be of supreme importance (see Gary Poll, "A Dozen Ideas on Teaching the Book of Mormon with Power," *CES Symposium,* August 1997). What is the message? As I understand it, the message is that Jesus suffered and died for us, and if we will keep his commandments and always remember him, we can have his Spirit to be with us. Maybe there are more messages within the prayer. Would you listen next time so you can hear them? And would you ponder them during the quiet time of the sacrament? That is my main hope in writing this chapter.

When we renew our baptismal covenant, the Lord also renews his covenant with us. Elder George Q. Cannon taught: "When we went forth into the waters of baptism and covenanted with our Father in heaven to serve Him and keep His commandments, He bound Himself also by covenant to us that He would never desert us, never leave us to ourselves, never forget us, that in the midst of trials and hardships, when everything was arrayed against us, He would be near unto us and would sustain us" (*Gospel Truth,* Vol. 1, 170).

My favorite time at church is during the sacrament. I like to make it my "personal review time." I know where I'll be every Sunday, and I know I'll have that time again to ask myself some important questions: Am I remembering the Savior always? Am I keeping his commandments? How can I do better next week?

Elder Jeffrey R. Holland made a suggestion to the young men of the Church: "May I suggest that wherever possible a white shirt be worn by the deacons, teachers, and priests who handle the sacrament. For sacred ordinances in the Church we often use ceremonial clothing, and a white shirt could be seen as a gentle reminder of the white clothing you wore in the baptismal font and an anticipation of the white shirt you will soon wear into the temple and onto your missions" (*Ensign,* November 1995, 68).

Of course, Elder Holland didn't call this a commandment; he said, "May I suggest . . ." He explained that he would like the deacons and priests to be mostly concerned about the purity of their lives. But, hey, when an Apostle of the Lord even makes a *suggestion*—the chosen generation listens. And that's you. Make the sacrament a time to remember the Savior and renew our commitment to remember him. C is for Covenants.

H IS FOR HOLY GHOST

Another reason we go to church is to feel the influence of the Holy Ghost. The Spirit makes things clear. It pulls us upward. It brings to our mind things we can do to be better. It's not just the speakers' and teachers' job to invite the Spirit. It's ours too. Elder Bruce R. McConkie said: "Both teacher and student must be in tune. I suspect that many of you sometime or other, probably in high school, took a course in physics and had laboratory experiments and used a tuning fork. You remember an occasion when two tuning forks were selected which were calibrated on the same wavelength, and one of them was set up in one part of the room, and the other thirty or forty feet away. Someone struck the first tuning fork, and people put their ear to the second, and it vibrated and made the same sound that came from the first one" (*Doctrines of the Restoration,* 333).

That demonstrates what is meant by "being in tune." If we are on the same wavelength as the Lord, our spirit will "vibrate"; we will *feel* the truth of what is being said. When we are sitting in our classes or our sacrament meetings, eager to feel the Spirit, listening intently for the Lord's instructions for us, we can experience what is promised in Doctrine and Covenants 50:22: "Wherefore, he that preacheth and he that receiveth, understand one another, and both are edified and rejoice together."

"Rejoicing together" with our friends and neighbors is what it's all about.

This next Sunday, why not set a goal to do all you can to prepare to feel the Spirit? I believe the Lord would like us to have that experience, but we can't if we aren't prepared. If we show up to church sleepy, disinterested, and bored, then we don't deserve to feel the Spirit.

After Jesus taught the Nephites, he told them to "go ye unto your homes, and ponder upon the things which I have said, and ask of the Father, in my name, that ye may understand, and *prepare your minds for the morrow,* and I come unto you again" (3 Nephi 17:3; emphasis added). There are so many things we can do to "prepare our minds" for our meetings! We can get enough sleep, we can read the Sunday School reading assignment, we can pray for our teachers and speakers in our prayers on Saturday night! It's all up to you.

If everybody did this, there wouldn't be any more bored people at church. Can we do it? Sure we can. We've been told that we are a chosen generation, now we can show it through our actions. How? Well, among other things, we'll choose to enjoy the meetings, honor the Sabbath, be unified with our brothers and sisters, respect those who teach us, thoughtfully renew our covenants, and strive to feel the influence of the Holy Ghost. Make your Sundays special, and the time you spend in church will become the best three hours of the week.

John Bytheway was born and reared in Salt Lake City, Utah, and is the fifth of six children. He served his mission in the Philippines, and later graduated from BYU. John has done lots of exciting things, but he wants you to know that he is a seminary graduate, a returned missionary, and he married in the temple. He highly recommends all three.

8

"ALL THESE THINGS SHALL GIVE THEE EXPERIENCE"

Sue Egan

There was an hour layover before my flight. The phone call earlier that evening from my husband, Rick, was still resonating in my mind.

"There's been an accident. It's Nathan. He was hit by a car while he was riding his bike." Rick's voice had cracked with emotion. "Nate's unconscious and has a severe head injury. He was taken by Life Flight to the hospital a couple of hours ago, and the doctors still can't stop the hemorrhaging. We can't even see him for a moment to give him a blessing until he's more stable. It doesn't look good. How soon can you be here?" The first of two flights was over and I was halfway there, but home seemed a million miles away.

I began to shake uncontrollably. Tears streamed down my cheeks. Desperately needing someone to talk to, I scanned the crowd that was also waiting at the gate for the flight to Salt Lake. Not expecting to see anyone familiar, I was instead searching for a countenance that I felt could be trusted. Dismissing face after face in the mass of strangers, I finally saw a young man who appeared to be about eighteen or nineteen years old, just about the age of our son Nathan. His pure expression was the first thing to catch my eye, then looking closer I saw that he was wearing one of our EFY T-shirts. Quickly making my way across the room, I introduced myself and told him that for the last five days I had been serving as the session director for EFY on the Northern Arizona University campus in Flagstaff. He told me that his name was Jake Allen. He lived in Arizona and was flying to Utah to spend a few days with his older sister. Grasping his hand, I tearfully began to unfold the sketchy details about Nate's accident and my desire to get to his bedside while he was still alive. Jake seemed very at ease speaking to me, and we conversed for a few minutes before the flight attendant came over and offered me early seating on the plane.

Fifteen minutes later, the same mass of adults that I had scanned for support at the gate area began to board the plane. Among the group was Jake. As he came to my row, I asked him if he would be willing to sit by me for the flight home. He readily agreed and for the next hour and a half Jake and I spoke with the ease of old friends. At times I would choke with emotion, yet Jake remained calm and continued to converse with me. As the plane landed in Salt Lake I thanked Jake for his support and handed him my card with our home phone number on it, assuring him that if he called, someone in the family could update him on Nathan's condition.

Within a few minutes after getting off the plane, I arrived at the L.D.S. Hospital and was escorted to the Intensive Care Unit to see Nate. Entering his room, I experienced a wave of peace that enfolded me, and I felt as if I were walking on sacred ground despite the scene before me. Nathan was lying motionless on the hospital bed. Machines hummed, catheters drained blood and fluid from his body, other tubes were delivering solutions and medication. A large tube protruding from his mouth fed oxygen to his lungs from the life support machine that was breathing for him. Several lines were attached to his chest, monitoring his heart. A nurse was at his bedside adjusting the IV solutions that were draining into his body. Amidst this maze of tubes and wires, Nathan lay still and unconscious, in a deep coma.

Details of the accident and injuries followed: " . . . hit by a car while crossing at a crosswalk on his bike . . . car traveling 45–55 mph . . . landed on his back on the car's windshield . . . thrown to the pavement . . . immediately curled up in fetal position on road . . . bleeding from nose, ears, and mouth . . . unconscious at the scene . . . Life Flight . . . doubtful he would survive five-minute flight to hospital . . . hemorrhaging from severe back lacerations . . . broken ribs . . . punctured lung . . . broken scapula . . . possible cracked vertebra . . . severe head trauma . . . brain damage . . . deep coma . . . prognosis uncertain. . . . "

Hours went by as our family remained at Nate's side. One of the nurses finally suggested that we go home and get some sleep. Before Rick took the children home, our family gathered around Nathan's bed, held hands, and offered the first of many emotional, humble, heartfelt pleas to Heavenly Father. As I stayed by his bedside throughout the night my mind reflected back on the seventeen years since Nate joined our family.

Nate is the third of six children. He has been autistic since birth. Much of our family time and energy had been spent on Nate, and he had been able to function quite well despite his handicap. Through the efforts of special-education teachers and other specialists, plus hours, days, weeks, and years of follow-through by family members, Nate learned to read, write, carry on conversations, ride the public transit system alone, work at a job, shop at the mall, and "hang out" with friends and cousins. He loved to work and could labor for hours and hours without tiring. He took a lot of pleasure in saving money and hoped to move to an apartment after his senior year of high school. He was well on his way to living a somewhat independent lifestyle. Our lifelong labor of love in teaching Nate to become self-supporting had begun to come to fruition. And now, this.

On the second day, the CAT scan revealed that Nathan's brain was bleeding in 25 different places. That was ten more than the day before. The nurses in the ICU saw accidents like this daily, and they began to prepare us for the possibilities. We were told that euthanasia wasn't legal in the United States but that we had the right to withhold feeding if the brain damage turned out to be so severe that Nate would never function again. Donating his organs was mentioned. Many people's lives were hanging in the balance while waiting for needed organs to keep them alive. If Nathan were to take a turn for the worse, that might be an option to consider. Long-term nursing home care was also discussed. It was possible that we would need someone to change his diapers, feed him through the tube, roll him over several times a day, and keep him comfortable for the years to come.

During the time we were at the hospital with Nate, our neighbors exemplified the baptismal covenant to "bear one another's burdens, that they might be light; . . . and mourn with those that mourn; yea, and comfort those that stand in need of comfort" (Mosiah 18:8–9). Our family was the recipient of hundreds of hours of service. Food was brought in, offers were abundant to care for our youngest child, Ali, the lawn was mowed and trimmed, the house was cleaned, a birthday cake was brought in for Nathan's younger brother, Taylor, and cards and letters filled the mailbox. After writing the first one hundred thank-you notes, we lost count of the many contributions and services. Spiritual needs were met as well. The entire ward held a fast for Nathan. The stake center was full the evening they met to break the fast and hear our dear bishop, Mike Gardner, pray for Nate. Nate's priest quorum and other members of the stake remembered him in their prayers, as did congregations of other denominations.

There was a steady stream of concerned family members, friends, and acquaintances flowing through the hospital waiting room, anxious to show their support.

Our extended family took turns sitting by Nate's bedside, so others could take a break for an hour or two. His Aunt Mary hung a banner on his hospital room wall that was also covered with pictures of aunts, uncles, and cousins. It read, "We Love Nathan!" Other family pictures were displayed in the room, along with Nate's favorite *Star Wars* paraphernalia. Our favorite doctor, Dr. Davis, had placed a small action-figure of Luke Skywalker, one of Nate's special heroes, in Nate's hand. Throughout his coma, Nate clasped that special, well-worn toy. The word *gratitude* took on a deepened meaning for us as the services rendered became literally life renewing, both physically and spiritually.

One afternoon, fifteen days into the coma, all but two of our immediate family members were gathered around Nate's bed. The breathing tube had been removed an hour earlier, and Nate was breathing on his own for the first time since the accident. Suddenly, Nate opened his eyes. Cautiously leaning over his bed I asked him if he wanted some ice. He nodded yes! After swallowing the small ice chip, Nathan whispered, "I want some more." We were elated! The nurse asked him if he knew any of the people surrounding his bed. He looked at each of our faces. As he saw his oldest sister he stared at her for a moment, then awkwardly pointed his finger and whispered, "Jennifer." We cried tears of joy and hugged one another as nurses and technicians began to pour into his room. We jammed the phone lines frantically making calls from the hospital, sharing the miraculous news, "Nate's awake!!!" We finally had our Nathan, or at least part of him, back once again.

The road to recovery was long and arduous. Nate was like a six-foot-tall infant. He had to relearn how to roll over, hold up his head, sit up, stand, and use his arms and legs once again. Over the weeks, we had to feed him by hand, taking care all the while to avoid his flailing arms.

It took three adults to periodically lift him off the bed and try to coach his legs into making walking movements. During these sessions, Nate would scream out in pain due to his broken rib and shoulder, which were not yet healed. He was also frustrated by his injured brain's inability to coordinate his movements. All this was almost unbearable to watch, and any progress that he was making seemed minuscule and laborious. Learning to speak again was one of the most difficult parts of his rehabilitation. He struggled to identify even the most familiar objects and quite often couldn't say the names of his closest friends and relatives.

He remained in the hospital for weeks as he tried to relearn basic life skills so that he could return to our home with some degree of function. Finally, after he had spent fifty-six days in the hospital, we prepared to take Nathan home. He would finish the ensuing months of therapy as an outpatient.

Nate has gone through months of very difficult rehabilitation. He missed his senior year of high school. His hope to get an apartment is now on hold, perhaps indefinitely. He can work a little, but he has only a fraction of the ability and attention span that he had before the accident. He has learned to walk, converse, read a little, and he still loves *Star Wars*. Our extended family continues to nurture him with outings and overnight stays in their homes. Each evening Nate visits the dozens of neighbors that open their households to him. In our eyes our neighborhood rivals that of Enoch, and we feel blessed beyond measure by their generosity.

Perhaps one of the most touching visits came a few months after the accident. My "good Samaritan" from the airport, Jake Allen, called the day he went into the MTC in preparation for a full-time mission to the Dominican Republic. He was in Salt Lake with his family and wanted to know if he could stop by and meet Nathan. As Nate and Jake embraced and then began visiting, his mother confided in me how shy Jake is around adults. How could that be? He had seemed to be so comfortable and helpful during our flight just a few months before. Clearly, the Lord had magnified Jake's ability to help when the need arose. That singular experience became an added testimony to Jake that the Lord would continue to magnify and bless him on his mission as he remained worthy and willing to serve others.

I share these experiences with Nate because the lessons learned apply to each of us. Take a moment and think of the greatest adversity you have in your life. Maybe your challenge is that your parents are divorced or possibly someone you love isn't living the gospel. Perhaps you are unbearably lonely or you have prayed for countless hours for something that still isn't happening. The examples are endless. Think of yours. Chances are whatever your trial is you have felt disappointment, fear, or even anger. Those are common emotions that accompany hardships. But it is how you respond to those feelings that makes all the difference. What does Heavenly Father tell us to do? Let's look at the words of the Lord to Joseph Smith during the time when the Prophet was going through a discouraging time in Liberty Jail. The Lord responded to the Prophet's cries by saying, "All these things shall give thee experience, and shall be for thy good" (D&C 122:7). That applies to us also. But what is required of us?

The key lies in our answer to the following question: "Have I softened or hardened my heart as a result of my trial?" If we are to fully benefit from the sanctifying lessons of adversity we must soften our hearts and move toward our Heavenly Father rather than away from him. We may be tempted to do otherwise, for Satan hopes that we will be embittered by the things we are called upon to endure. He hopes that the feelings of anger, frustration, and fear will stimulate us to rebel against Heavenly Father. He wants us to believe that our Heavenly Father doesn't really love us or He would not allow this bad thing to happen. He hopes that we give up trying to be righteous and instead fall into paths of sin. He desires that we become unreachable and unteachable, left to wallow forever in feelings of hopelessness and despair. He would like us to believe that we'll never really feel the love of our Heavenly Father again.

Don't fall for Satan's lies. The words of the Apostle Paul are true. He testifies, "Who shall separate us from the love of Christ? Shall tribulation, or distress, or persecution, or famine, or nakedness, or peril, or sword? . . . Nay, in all these things we are more than conquerors through him that loved us. For I am persuaded, that neither death, nor life, . . . nor powers, nor things present, nor things to come, nor height, nor depth, nor any other creature, shall be able to separate us from the love of God, which is in Christ Jesus our Lord" (Romans 8:35–39). As we soften our heart, remain faithful, and come unto Christ, we will feel his love even when encompassed by trials. I bear witness of that.

Our blessings extend far beyond experiencing his divine, wonderful, perfect love. When our hearts are soft not only will we feel our Savior's love for us, but he will also teach us. When the path before us is uncertain, he will tell us where to put our feet, for he has promised, "I will lead you along" (D&C 78:18). And as we travel that path with him we will learn about things such as patience, trust, faith, long-suffering, gratitude, charity, consecration, and other lessons we would never learn if left to ourselves. If we could see things as they really are, we would express appreciation for those trials that are too difficult for us to handle on our own for when we humble ourselves, "even in the depths of humility, calling on the name of the Lord daily, . . . [we] shall always rejoice, and be filled with the love of God, . . . and [we] shall grow . . . in the knowledge of that which is just and true" (Mosiah 4:11–12). This is a blessing that is a hundred times greater than any sacrifice we are required to make. Heavenly Father is so generous with us!

Through the experience of mothering Nathan I am coming to know God and his son Jesus Christ in a very real and powerful way. I love the Lord and trust his plan even when the way appears uncertain and impassable, for he has truly "led me along." I want to be his forever. May each of us take this divine counsel to heart, "I would that ye should be steadfast and immovable, always abounding in good works, that Christ, the Lord God Omnipotent, may seal you his, that you may be brought to heaven, that ye may have everlasting salvation and eternal life" (Mosiah 5:15).

Sue Egan is a homemaker from Salt Lake City, Utah. She and her husband, Rick, are the parents of six children: Jennifer, Spencer, Nathan, Joshua, Taylor, and Allison. Sue has served in a variety of Church callings, including ward and stake Young Women president and five times as Primary music leader. She loves reading the scriptures (especially the Book of Mormon) and delights in sharing the gospel with anyone who will listen.

9

PRESSURE POINTERS

Brad Wilcox

I wish my parents would try to understand how really hard it is for an LDS teenager," writes Tristen from Tennessee. "It's hard to be everything we're expected to be with all the peer pressure there is to break the Word of Wisdom, to break house family rules, and to even break the law. Sometimes kids would rather be dead than different. And then we are pushed at home to get good grades and be responsible around the house. Sometimes it's so hard that I just want to lie down and sleep."

Do teens have pressure and stress in their lives? The answer is a resounding yes! What pressures? There are as many different answers to this question as there are people who feel pressured. But, quite simply, pressures are any external force that influences us. Such forces may come from friends, school, media, and any change in our lives, however minor. Stress is an internal reaction to those outside pressures, and stress affects our health and happiness.

It is important to remember that though we usually speak of pressure and stress in negative ways, they are a vital part of why we were sent to earth. Positive influences, such as those provided by the Church, good friends, and family, help us progress and improve. Stress can keep us motivated and productive. It often allows us to concentrate, focus, and perform at peak efficiency. Without it, we would likely become pretty bored and frustrated.

Pressure and stress are unavoidable facts of life. It is how we handle them that makes them positive or negative. When the heat is on, do we see it as a refiner's fire or just let it burn us out?

Remember the movie *The Wizard of Oz?* Dorothy found herself traveling a road that led through an unfamiliar world. She encountered many challenges and problems, but she also found three friends to share the journey and help her find her way home—Scarecrow, Tin Man, and Lion. Many young people today are in much the same situation as Dorothy. You are trying to follow a straight and narrow path through a world filled with opposition and wicked witches.

In the movie, Scarecrow wanted a brain, which would help him think; Tin Man wanted a heart, which would allow him to show emotions, such as love and laughter; and Lion wanted courage, which would make him brave. As we deal with pressure and stress, we must learn to think things through and manage stress appropriately. We must learn to exhibit emotions associated with the heart, including a sense of humor. And we can find personal courage to face problems through learning about and emulating worthy heroes.

GET A BRAIN

Think about managing stress. When I was in graduate school, my wife and I often felt overwhelmed. As we mapped out one week's schedule, we frequently said, "Okay, we'll just have to take it one thing at a time." We chuckled one evening when our daughter, who was in fourth grade then, pulled her homework out of her backpack and sighed, "I'll just have to take it one thing at a time."

The ability to think through a problem and generate solutions does not always come naturally. It takes experiences and practice to break a problem down into parts, focus on the most important parts first, and then solve the problem, one step at a time. How many of us think about the consequences of our actions ahead of time? If I am tempted to lower my moral standards and give time to fantasies, for example, I must also take time to think of the other moments that are sure to follow—not fantasies at all. Everyone loves to watch fireworks on the Fourth of July, but few consider that on the fifth of July someone has to clean up the mess. Elder M. Russell Ballard explains, "We must govern our actions every day with our future in mind. One of Satan's clever tactics is to tempt us to concentrate on the present and ignore the future" (*Ensign*, November 1990, 36).

Do you realize that simply by living the Word of Wisdom, Latter-day Saints already have a huge jump on others when it comes to stress management? One article claimed the three best ways to reduce stress are to stop smoking, limit the intake of caffeine, and drink no more than four alcoholic drinks per week. Another article reported results of studies indicating that those who worship regularly in church settings and take personal time each day for such things as scripture study and prayer are better able to manage stress, control their tempers, and actually live longer.

There are also other ways to deal with stress. Do we know how to relax by taking a break? Do we know how to appropriately escape for a while and have some fun? Do we know how to organize our time? Many of the pressures that come up and cause stress in our lives might be avoided with a little advanced planning.

HAVE A HEART

One of the best ways to find heart is through humor. Susan and Joe Shumway, with their family of six small children, had been vacationing in Mexico. Joe's work required him to return to their home in Laramie, Wyoming, a few days early, and Susan, pregnant with number seven, found herself shepherding her brood

through customs and having to deal with mounting dis-
tractions and problems. "There I was," she recalls, "out of
money and out of diapers. I was trying to keep track of all
the luggage and all the children at the same time. I was so
pregnant I could hardly walk." The man at the customs
counter looked from Susan to her six noisy charges and
back to Susan. "Lady, go right on through," he invited. "If
you have drugs in those bags, you need them." A humorous viewpoint, a shared laugh, and Susan's journey
became more bearable, so bearable, in fact, that Susan and
Joe have since added children numbers eight and nine.
Nine children can cause a lot of stress, but Susan and Joe
have learned to handle it.

A headline on a national magazine cover read, "Reduce
Stress: Laugh!" The accompanying article related medical
studies linking laughter with better physical and mental
health. As Susan experienced that day in the airport,
shared humor helps people get beyond the ugly and frus-
trating, endure the difficult, deal with the unexpected, and
bear the unbearable. Humor helps. Humor heals. As we are
told in Ecclesiastes, there is "a time to laugh" (3:4).

President Hugh B. Brown once said, "A wholesome
sense of humor will be a safety valve that will enable you
to apply the lighter touch to heavy problems and learn
some lessons in problem-solving that 'sweat and tears'
often fail to dissolve" (in Conference Report, April 1968,
100).

A teenager attending Education Week one year had hair
that was trimmed nicely, except for one swatch down the
center of his head that must have been at least a foot long.
I called him my "three-fourths missionary" and asked
what he was going to do with the long hair when he
entered the Missionary Training Center. The young man
replied, "My mom is going to have a big party and invite
the ward. Then she'll cut it off, frame it, and call it 'free
agency.'"

My friend Douglas Bassett told me about a student in
his seminary class who felt nervous because she had not

studied for a test on pregnancy and prenatal development for her health class. She surprised herself by doing better than she expected on the test. In fact, she was so excited when she got on the school bus that afternoon that she yelled across the bus to her friend, "Hey, Sarah, I passed my pregnancy test!"

President James E. Faust once counseled a young couple he was sealing in the Salt Lake Temple to develop humor. He told them that when he blessed children, including his own, he always blessed them with a sense of humor, hoping that it would help them find balance in their lives, guard against becoming too rigid, and keep their problems and difficulties in perspective. He counseled the couple that if laughter was not a natural gift for them, they would do well to work at developing a healthy sense of humor (see BYU Devotional, March 17, 1981).

For those who are not fortunate enough to have been blessed as infants by President Faust or reared in a home in which a sense of humor was fostered, a sense of humor can be nurtured. Barbara Barrington Jones confirms, "Believe it or not, humor can be developed. I am living proof of that fact" (*The Confident You,* 1992, 139). Sister Jones's father was an accountant, and her mother taught etiquette in a private girls' school; the home in which she was reared was quiet and orderly, and decorum reigned. But when Sister Jones grew up and she and her husband joined the Church, she found that decorum wasn't necessarily a cure for all her needs. She was asked to present workshops for teenagers at youth conferences, and she claims her first attempts were disasters. "I was a sleeping pill!" she says.

She was advised, "Try to remember back to when you were their age. Think of humorous experiences in your own life that youth can relate to." Lacking a personal background of humorous experiences, Sister Jones began searching for humor. She started to keep a notebook in which she wrote down fun things that she experienced or heard. For example, she attended a general conference session in which President Thomas S. Monson told of a letter

that President Ezra Taft Benson had received after under-
going heart surgery: "Dear President Benson, I know that
you will be blessed for this surgery because in the Bible it
says 'blessed are the pacemakers.'" With a smile, Sister
Jones wrote this incident down in her notebook. Another
heartfelt touch of humor was mentioned by a General
Authority who described a handmade, get-well card he
received while recovering from bypass surgery. On the
front of the card the child, a second grader, had drawn a
long, black, rectangular box, representing a coffin, with a
long flower poking out of the center. Inside he had printed
in big letters, "Hope you get well soon, but if not, have
fun!" After a hearty laugh, Sister Jones wrote down that
account as well. Thanks to her notebook, Sister Jones col-
lected a number of examples she could use in talks and
presentations, and, at the same time, sharpened her ability
to recognize humor. Now she relates beautifully to the
young people to whom she speaks.

President Gordon B. Hinckley has said, "We need to
have a little humor in our lives. We better take seriously
that which should be taken seriously, but at the same time
we can bring in a touch of humor now and again. If the
time ever comes when we can't smile at ourselves, it will
be a sad time" (Interview with Michael Cannon of the
Church News, September 1, 1995).

Have you ever wondered if God has a sense of humor?
Heber C. Kimball taught, "I am perfectly satisfied that my
Father and my God is a cheerful, pleasant, lively, and
good-natured being . . . . He is a jovial, lively person, and a
beautiful man" (in *Journal of Discourses,* 4:222).

When you face pressure and stress, try to laugh, step
back, and laugh again. Remember, if you can laugh at it,
you can live with it.

TAKE COURAGE

One of the most effective ways to learn courage is from
worthy heroes. Who are the heroes young people look up
to? *People* magazine, for 27 June 1992, reported that the

top teen idols of all time were (1) the Beatles, who John Lennon described in 1966 as "more popular than Jesus," (2) Madonna, who was quoted as saying, "I saw losing my virginity as a career move," and (3) Elvis Presley, who died of debauchery and a drug overdose.

No wonder one young woman said, "Being a total hero isn't possible in today's society." In a special summer/fall 1990 issue of *Newsweek,* a popular movie maker reportedly said, "I believe that we are at a fairly frightening, transitional stage of history. We tried the Ozzie-and-Harriet thing in the 50s, and that didn't work. Then we tried the hippie peace-and-love thing, and that didn't work either. Then we tried the yuppie thing, and the world got worse. So what's next? Today, there is no clear way for teenagers to go. All they have are politicians, TV preachers, and cynical heavy-metal musicians telling them things that they sense are lies. No one is offering them the truth they crave so deeply."

I wholeheartedly disagree. Today there is a clear way for teenagers to go, and beyond the counterfeits and media-hyped imitations, there are worthy heroes to be found and followed. Many in the world may not recognize it, accept it, or appreciate it, but "the truth they crave so deeply" has been restored and is readily available. We can find worthy heroes within the Church and in the pages of the scriptures. We can fill our bedroom walls with pictures of these heroes.

At one youth conference in California, I asked the teenagers to tell me what pictures they had hanging on the walls of their bedrooms. Some said they had athletes; others mentioned rock stars and movie stars. I then talked about selecting worthy heroes. After the conference a letter of thanks came from one of the leaders. However, the words that meant the most to me were not written in the letter, but across the back of the envelope: "P.S. Remember the new convert you met named Billy? I saw him in the LDS bookstore yesterday buying pictures of the apostles and Book of Mormon characters to put on his bedroom walls."

One of my greatest heroes when I was growing up was

President Spencer W. Kimball. I will never forget the thrill it was to meet him before my mission. I was touring in the cast of the LDS musical *My Turn on Earth,* and we received word that President Kimball was going to bring members of his family to the play for family home evening. I was worried about it all week. You see, I played the part of Satan, which meant I would be portraying the devil in front of the prophet. What if he told me I did a good job?

At the time, my Church calling was teaching the twelve-year-olds in Sunday School. I asked the members of my class what they would say to President Kimball if they had the chance to meet him. One boy said, "I'd ask him if he has to wear make-up in general conference." Another said he would ask if he wanted to go water skiing with him the next summer. Finally, a Lamanite girl said, "If I had the chance to meet President Kimball, I'd just tell him that I love him."

After the play the next evening, the members of the cast were invited into a backstage room to meet President Kimball and some members of his family. The production manager introduced me as Elder Wilcox, because I was in the process of sending in my mission papers.

President Kimball said, "Oh, Elder Wilcox, where are you going on your mission?"

"I don't know," I said. "I thought you knew."

President Kimball laughed and asked, "What are you doing in the Church right now?"

I said, "I teach the twelve-year-olds in Sunday School."

President Kimball said, "There's no more important calling in the Church. What did you teach them yesterday?"

I couldn't remember. All I could recall at that moment was asking them what they would say if they had the chance to meet a prophet face-to-face. So I said, "President Kimball, I asked them what they would say if they had the opportunity to meet you."

"And what did they tell you?"

I smiled and said, "They told me that they would tell you they love you. I love you." And that's when he held me. He didn't just hug me, he held me for several moments. I will never forget the love I felt.

Young people, you don't need to meet a prophet to find a worthy hero. There are many very close to home. In Proverbs 4:18 we read, "The path of the just is as the shining light." A young man from Toronto, Canada, said, "Nothing gives me more courage to stand up to the pressures around me like knowing someone else is doing it too. I say to myself, 'If he can do it, then I can too.'"

Amy, a seventeen-year-old from Pleasanton, California, said, "My parents are my heroes. Their example makes me want to do what's right." One young man, Reid, from Plano, Texas, also found a hero in his father. This seventeen-year-old wrote, "My dad told me that he had never touched a cigarette in his whole life and if I were to decide to try smoking he wanted me to invite him, and he would smoke for the first time too. Because of that, I still have never touched a cigarette, and I never will."

Another young man wrote, "Life becomes so much easier as I draw nearer to Heavenly Father and Jesus Christ. They have done, and are doing, so much for me. I know that Jesus Christ died for me and that if I were the only person on the earth, he still would have done what he did—just for me." As my friend Kenneth Cope wrote in song, there is "never a better hero" than the Savior ("Greater Than Us All," Embryo Records, 1989). The Lord is our ultimate example and guide, and he loves and will help every one of us discover our true courage.

Just as in *The Wizard of Oz,* if we can learn to think our problems through, to gain heart by using humor, and to find courage through the lives of worthy heroes, we will have the support we need to continue down the road of life and ultimately make it home.

But wait! There is another character in the story we are forgetting—Toto, Dorothy's dog. In fact, Toto is the driving force throughout the movie. Interestingly enough, the word *toto* means total, complete, whole.

It is not enough to use intellect alone when dealing

with the pressures and stress that confront us. Heart by itself is also insufficient. Courage without thought and feeling could end up causing more problems than it helps to solve. The goal that should drive us through the plots of our lives is the wise and sensitive combination of all these elements.

There are lots of lions and tigers and bears out there. There are lots of wicked witches too. By being smart, happy, and brave we can overcome them all with our goodness. As we progress along our path in life, we must not forget to take along the Scarecrow, Tin Man, the Lion, and as Dorothy says in the movie—"Toto, too."

Brad Wilcox was born and reared in Provo, Utah, apart from childhood years spent in Ethiopia, Africa. He served a mission to Chile and later married Debi Gunnell. They have four children. Brad is an assistant professor in the Department of Teacher Education at Brigham Young University where he also serves as campus adviser to the Golden Key National Honor Society and director of the Student Teaching and Intern Program in Central America. Brad loves raspberry/blackberry frozen yogurt and homemade root beer. He also enjoys writing for Church magazines and has even been quoted in Reader's Digest.

10

JOSEPH SMITH, THE RESTORATION, AND YOU

Scott Anderson

One early winter day, the doorway of my office was filled up almost completely by one of my students—a member of the high school football team. He looked somewhat bewildered, so I asked if there was anything I could do to help. He admitted that there was. The girl's choice dance was coming up. His bewilderment was due to the fact that he had not yet been asked. "Who would they want to ask if they don't want to ask me?" he questioned. I told him that girls like humble guys like him, so I couldn't understand it either. He informed me that he and his friends really did want to know what the girls are looking for in a guy.

"So, why don't you just ask them?" I thought this would work quite well. "They might not tell us the whole truth, Brother Anderson. Why don't you ask them?" I could see his point and agreed to run an informal survey to find out what the young women were looking for in an ideal date.

A brief survey was typed to be delivered to about 400 LDS high-school-age young women. The title of the survey was "Your Perfect Man." The first question was, "How tall should he be?" The answers ranged from 5 foot 2 inches to 6 foot 10 inches. All the young men seemed to feel okay about that since they were all in the general range. The next question was, "How much should he weigh?" It was evident that some young women are unaware that a young man usually weighs more than a young woman does, even if they are the same height. For example, one answer said the perfect man was to be 6 feet tall, be "muscle-bound," and weigh 125 pounds! It was easy to see that we might have a few problems with the survey.

The next question was about neck size. Why would we ask neck size? Well, it was wrestling season, and as a young man works out on the mat, his neck starts to grow in size. A typical neck size might be 15 to 17 inches. One young lady said a 3-inch neck size would be preferable. I'm not sure, but I think that would be only the size of an esophagus and that's all. One young lady wrote, "I don't care just as long as he does" (we'll talk about that one another day.)

Next, we wanted to see if the young women wanted their ideal man to be rippling with muscles, so we asked about performance in a highly publicized exercise in our school—the bench press. The survey simply said, "Bench-press____ pounds." The young women were to fill in the blank. Young men can generally lift about the same as they weigh, then after conditioning and practice they are able to lift quite a bit more. Like the "400 Club" at BYU whose members can bench-press 400 pounds and could probably change the tire on a small car by picking up the car and taking off the wheel with their bare hands. Anyway, one young woman said that her ideal man would be able to bench-press about 25 pounds—which made all of us feel better about our abilities. One girl said she didn't care how many pounds, just as long as he did all the laundry. (We were to find out that she thought "bench-pressing" was a type of ironing, and she didn't care how many pounds it was—just do all of it!)

As we read through the surveys, it became obvious that some of the answers weren't relevant. But we got an overall picture of what the girls were looking for in the "perfect date." He would combine the physical attributes of "Gaston," in the movie *Beauty and the Beast* and possess the character traits of the "beast" after he had returned to being the prince. The ideal date would therefore be approximately the size of a barge, yet be unfailingly humble, thoughtful, kind, considerate, polite, respectful, and gentle.

As I shared the results of the survey with the young men they struggled a bit to understand how they could be both "strong" and "gentle," both "macho" and "humble"—and somehow keep it all in balance. We talked about Joseph Smith who is an example of a man who had achieved such balance. By any measure, the Prophet was an ideal specimen of a man. He was 6 feet, 2 inches tall, and in his day that was much taller than the average man. He weighed around 200 pounds and was unusually strong and agile (not to mention handsome). But at the same time, he was kind, thoughtful, and considerate. He was also a very spiritual man and a person of great integrity, one whom the Lord had raised up to open the dispensation of the fullness of times.

In seminary we will have the opportunity to study the miraculous story of how the gospel was restored, how the Doctrine and Covenants came about, and the great role the Prophet Joseph Smith played in bringing the truth to the earth again. I have a testimony of his divine foreordination and of his great courage, amazing humility, and endless faith. My prayer for you is that you will come to appreciate his tremendous example of devotion to the truth he loved and taught, and even gave his life for, and that this gratitude for the Prophet Joseph Smith and the Restoration can change your life.

Elder Neal A. Maxwell said, "With the Restoration came a clear understanding of who we are. . . . Isn't it marvelous to ponder how much the Prophet Joseph Smith learned throughout the extended process of restoring the holy priesthood, the holy endowment, the holy sealing power? But young Joseph, whose impact would become global, merely went into the Sacred Grove to find out which local church he should join! How generous God is!" (May 2, 1993 Priesthood Commemoration Fireside at Temple Square).

Because you have been saved to be part of the final

dispensation, your potential is unlimited! Elder Maxwell went on to say, "However, when you and I come to understand our true identities, God loves us too much to let us be content with what we have achieved spiritually up to now, because He is a perfect Father. He knows what we have the power to become, and He has His special ways of being lovingly insistent."

So how do we "come to understand our true identities"? How do we learn to follow the promptings of a loving Father in Heaven as he is being "lovingly insistent" that we become all we can be? With all I know, and with all my heart, I testify to you that as you study the life of the Prophet Joseph Smith and exercise your faith to try with all your might to live the Savior's teachings, you will find the answers to these questions and come to know your part in this—the final gospel dispensation.

LEARNING TO KNOW YOUR TRUE IDENTITY

One of the beautiful lessons taught in the First Vision came with the very first word our Heavenly Father spoke as he visited young Joseph. Imagine this young farm boy simply going to a grove to pray and suddenly having such a glorious vision unfolded before him. As the light descended and Joseph gazed into the loving faces of Deity, the first word he heard spoken to him was, "Joseph." Can any of us begin to imagine what it would be like to hear the God of all Creation, even our loving Heavenly Father, call us by name? The very God of Heaven and Earth was that aware of Joseph, one young boy. What a startling realization that the impersonal force for good he had always heard about from other professors of religion, was standing before him as a personal, loving, caring Heavenly Father. As soon as Joseph gained his composure he asked for the direction he came seeking. And what a marvelous light was restored to the earth from that very moment. How generous God is!

Not only did Joseph Smith learn that he was a child of God and that his Heavenly Father loved and cared for him, he also found out that there was a work for him to do. He began to glimpse what it meant to be here in the last days and to have been saved to do a great work in preparing for the Second Coming.

Are we allowing this light to come into our own lives? Think back on this morning, when you looked in the mirror. Did you smile at yourself and say, "Good morning, isn't it great to be me! I just can't wait to have another wonderful day!" Or was it more like, "Good morning, swamp witch! What happened to you overnight?" Maybe you sang your favorite hymn, "When upon life's *pillows* you are tempest-tossed, when you are discouraged, thinking all is lost!" Why does this happen? Is it because we have our morning prayer, "Good morning, Heavenly Father," and he answers, "Good morning, ugly child!" Can you imagine him saying, "Oh, I am sorry. I made a mistake when I created you, but just hang on, and I will correct it in the Resurrection!" Of course not! We know that Heavenly Father doesn't want us to feel that way. However, Nephi warns us that in the last days the adversary will whisper in our ears (see 2 Nephi 28:22) and teach us untruths. So what would happen if tomorrow morning when we heard those discouraging whispers from the wrong source—"You sure have an ugly body!"—we were to let the truth make us free and just say, "Oh, yeah? Well, you don't have a body at all!" Then ignore those lies. Yes, it is true that just as he tried with Joseph Smith, the adversary will try to get us to forget our destiny, put aside what we came here to do, and not allow the Lord's magnificent light to penetrate us. You, too, were saved for this wonderful day and have a glorious mission to fulfill. You were a valiant spirit in the premortal world and have been blessed with a marvelous destiny.

As we come to understand our true identities, our hearts and minds become open to the prompting of the Spirit, and our Father in Heaven can literally direct our actions as he did Joseph's. Joseph Smith learned his own true identity the very second Heavenly Father spoke to him in the Sacred Grove. I know that Heavenly Father knows *you* by name, too. He will give you guidance and direction as you seek it and learn to listen to his spirit.

LISTENING TO THE SPIRIT

Denice sat quietly in the back of the room. She seemed reluctant to leave. She kept feeling the prompting, and she felt she knew what she needed to do. But could she do it? She knew that Joseph Smith had found the courage to think of his mother's needs, and she understood that Nephi had found the courage, even when his father, Lehi, was murmuring, to go to his father for counsel. But her father was so far away from the Church and so disinterested. However, as she had listened that day in class to the account of the broken bow (see 1 Nephi 16) and listened as Lehi complained against God, and Nephi went to him *anyway,* the Spirit had plainly prompted her to reach out of her comfort zone and try to help her father. She was so busy in school and had so many other things to do, but she knew that in this time of her own great need, she should think of her father and try to find some way to help him. That night she prayed for strength to talk to her dad about the gospel. She was afraid of how he might respond, but she picked up the phone anyway, to call him in Canada. In their conversation, she finally found the courage to try. "Dad, thank you for caring about me so much. I just want you to know how much I love you. You are one of the people I trust deeply in my life. I am learning some wonderful things here at school. Some of them are about the Book of Mormon and the Church, and I would like to share them with you—"

Her father interrupted the conversation. "Denice, you know how I feel about that—let's talk about something else."

"But, Dad, I've always felt that it would be wonderful if I could have a blessing from you, since no one loves me like you do."

"Let's talk about something else!" he snapped. Their brief conversation ended and left her feeling frustrated and empty.

Three months later, after enjoying many more wonderful experiences with the scriptures, Denice was headed home for Christmas. She called her father the night before she was to leave. In their conversation she couldn't hold back and once again she asked, "Dad, while I am home for the Christmas break, can I share some of the things I have been learning about the Church?"

"You know how I feel about that," came her father's terse reply. She didn't know what to say. Then the silence was broken by her father's tearful confession. "I'm sorry Denice, I just can't wait until you get home to tell you. When you talked to me last September, it touched me so deeply, I went to see the bishop the next day. I finished project temple about two weeks ago, and last week I was ordained an elder. I have a present wrapped under the tree that is an offer to give you a father's blessing while you are home. Thank you, Denice. Thank you for wanting so much to share all this with me."

President Gordon B. Hinckley has said, "I have seen miracles in my time, my brothers and sisters. The greatest miracle of all, I believe, is the transformation that comes into the life of a man or a woman who accepts the restored gospel of Jesus Christ and tries to live it in his or her life. How thankful I am for the wonders of the restored gospel of Jesus Christ. It is indeed a marvelous work and a wonder which has been brought to pass by the power of the Almighty in behalf of His sons and daughters" (Address delivered at Vacaville/Santa Rosa, California, 21 May, 1995).

Just as Joseph Smith was richly rewarded for asking merely to know which local church to join, Denice was also generously blessed for having the courage to listen to the Spirit and ask her father for his blessing. Her life, the life of her father, and the life of her entire family will never be the same.

In February of 1847, when the Prophet Joseph appeared to him in a dream or vision, Brigham asked his predecessor if he had a message for the Brethren. The Prophet said: "Tell the people to be humble and faithful, and be sure to keep the Spirit of the Lord and it will lead them right. Be careful and not turn away the small still voice; it will teach you what to do and where to go; it will yield the fruits of the kingdom. Tell the brethren to keep their hearts open to conviction, so that when the Holy Ghost comes to them, their hearts will be ready to receive it."

The Prophet further directed Brigham Young as follows: "They can tell the Spirit of the Lord from all other spirits; it will whisper peace and joy to their souls; it will take malice, hatred, strife, and all evil from their hearts; and their whole desire will be to do good, bring forth righteousness and build up the kingdom of God" (Manuscript History of Brigham Young, 1846–1847, comp. Elden J. Watson, Salt Lake City [1971], 529).

Church history teaches how the Prophet Joseph Smith's whole desire was to bring forth righteousness and bring forth the kingdom of God against all opposition. He states: "From my boyhood until the present time I have been hunted like a roe upon the mountain. I have never been allowed to live like other men. I have been driven, chased, stoned, whipped, robbed, mobbed, imprisoned, persecuted, accused falsely of everything bad" (John Pulsipher, "Autobiography," typescript, BYU, 7).

One example follows: "Certain residents of Hyrum, Ohio, vented their personal feelings with mob action directed against the Prophet and Sidney Rigdon. Stimulated by whiskey and hidden behind blackened faces, a gang of more than two dozen men dragged Joseph from his bed during the night of March 24, 1832. Choking him into submission, they stripped him naked, scratched his skin with their fingernails, tore his hair, then smeared his body with tar and feathers. A vial of nitric acid forced against his teeth splashed on his face; a front tooth was broken. Meanwhile, other members of the mob dragged Rigdon by his heels from his home, bumping his head on the frozen ground, which left him delirious for days. The Prophet's friends spent the night removing the tar to help him keep a Sunday morning preaching appointment. He addressed a congregation that included Simonds Ryder, organizer of the mob" (James B. Allen and Glen M. Leonard, *The Story of the Latter-day Saints* [1992], 81).

FAITH TO FOLLOW THE SAVIOR

When I think how the Prophet preached the morning after this attack by the mob, I am overcome with gratitude for this example of "carrying on." Can we even imagine his bruised and welted body, burned and beaten, his face scarred from the night's ordeal, and with all this he was still able to speak of the joy of the gospel of Jesus Christ. How easily he could have pointed out his enemies sitting amongst them and then he could have turned his friends against them, but he would not. I am amazed at his forbearance, even with those who despised him. The Prophet Joseph truly followed the Savior in forgiving everyone—even his enemies.

W. W. Phelps, a friend of Joseph and Emma's, joined the Church but later apostatized. While living in Missouri, he and others signed a document that stated falsely that the Saints were in rebellion against the state. This document would come into the hands of Governor Boggs who would then issue the order to either exterminate or drive all Mormons from the state. There is no way to begin to describe what the Saints went through, in part because of the treachery of Phelps. Joseph was imprisoned for almost six months, Saints were killed, homes were burned, women attacked, the members of the Church were driven a distance of more than 240 miles, across a snow-swept prairie, and Joseph's family was driven from him. After the terrible trek, Emma records arriving at the Mississippi River and seeing it frozen over. The wagons drove across, but because of the fear of the ice breaking, she went upstream and braved her way by foot across the ice with a child hanging on each leg, a baby in each arm, and pages of the inspired version of the Bible sewn into her petticoats for protection. She knew if the ice broke, she and the children would be swept away to their deaths.

Following their expulsion from Missouri, the Saints would be forced to live in a malaria-infested swamp and so many would become very ill. As a result of W. W. Phelps's betrayal and the actions of others, untold suffering had come on Joseph and the members of the Church.

Some time later, after the most difficult persecution was past and the swamp had been drained and the city of Nauvoo was being built, W. W. Phelps wrote to Joseph to ask forgiveness for what he had done and request permission to return to the Church and the friendship of the Saints. Joseph replied: "You may in some measure realize what my feelings, as well as Elder Rigdon's and Brother Hyrum's were, when we read your letter—truly our hearts were melted into tenderness and compassion when we ascertained your resolves . . .

"Believing your confession to be real, and your repentance genuine, I shall be happy once again to give you the right hand of fellowship, and rejoice over the returning prodigal.

"Your letter was read to the Saints last Sunday, and an expression of their feeling was taken when it was unanimously *resolved,* That W. W. Phelps should be received into fellowship.

"'Come on, dear brother, since the war is past,
    For friends at first, are friends again at last.'
Yours as ever,
Joseph Smith Jun." (*History of the Church,* 4:163–64).

W. W. Phelps later wrote the hymn "Praise to the Man" as a tribute to Joseph Smith and was one of the principal speakers at the Prophet's funeral, where he stood and wept as he described the forgiveness he had been granted by this great prophet of God.

Joseph learned to follow the Spirit with exactness. For his love of the Savior and his sacrifice for the gospel, Joseph Smith deserves all the "praise" we can give him. There is no greater tribute given any other mortal man than that recorded in Section 135 of the Doctrine and Covenants, where it says, "Joseph Smith, the Prophet and

Seer of the Lord, has done more, save Jesus only, for the salvation of men in this world, than any other man that ever lived in it" (v. 3).

As Joseph was approaching the martyrdom, he again reminds us of those things that matter most. The morning he left Nauvoo for Carthage, he returned home three times to hug his children, hold his wife, and express his love to them. His family was so greatly important to him. He loved his children and was a great father. He adored his wife and was an excellent husband. He cared so deeply for his mother and father and brothers and sisters. I have admired young people I have known who have followed Joseph's great example in this regard.

I once watched a young woman, who was leaving with her boyfriend on their way to a movie, return to the house to invite her little brother to come along. How loved and important he must have felt as he enjoyed that evening with the couple. I have felt the power of a wonderful son who when he was young started the tradition of hugging everyone in the family "good night." As he was dropped off at the MTC and his happy but somewhat lonely parents returned home and prepared for bed, his mother quietly said, "I am going to miss that big boy's hug tonight," only to turn down the covers and find a note pinned on the pillows that said, "Here is your hug for tonight!" Thank you, wonderful youth, for the love you show for your families.

So why was Joseph like this, and why are there youth today that are such examples of great faith? The answer is that they all have the same hero, Jesus Christ. He, the Perfect Man, provided the greatest example of love ever known. Not that long ago, really, he left that upper room with his disciples after they had sung a hymn. He left all but three disciples outside the Garden. The three came in, and he asked for their prayers. He went a little way off and fell on his face, enduring a type of spiritual suffering and agony so great that there is no way to express it. Those drops of blood, which came from every pore, were shed for you and me. He didn't need to atone for himself. He was perfect. And so, it was an act of perfect selflessness. He could have stopped at any moment. The suffering would have ended any mortal's life, but he would not yet die, for his work was not complete.

Think of it. Hours of suffering, then the betrayal by a trusted friend, being mocked, spit upon, scourged, belittled, and tortured by a crown of cruel thorns. He could have ended any or all of it at any moment, yet he went on to endure the horrors of crucifixion, with the awful spikes and wrenching pain. How unbelievable is it that he would plead in behalf of his tormentors, "Father, forgive them; for they know not what they do"? (Luke 23:34). Consider the hours, the pain, and then the loneliness: "My God, my God, why hast thou forsaken me?" (Matthew 27:46). Would the Atonement have been complete without the Savior experiencing the spiritual loneliness we feel when we sin—when the Spirit leaves us because we are not worthy of it? He, though sinless, hung alone as all heaven wept. He knows spiritual loneliness, and he will be there for us so that we need never be alone. Finally, when it was complete, his great heart burst, and his immortal spirit left his body. He left this life with a heart broken for us. I love him so much. I know he lives. He is our Hero. He is the Perfect Man.

Scott Anderson and his wife, Angelle, live in Bluffdale, Utah, where they spend time working on home improvement projects, waiting for their children to come to family meetings, and ordering pizza as a reward for cleaning the house. He likes to travel, and his favorite places to go are to Florida and Georgia to see his married children and darling grandchildren. His hobbies include writing, farming, working on the house, the outdoors and all kinds of sports (especially football), and building memories with his family. He has a Ph.D. in Marriage and Family Therapy from BYU and is currently on the faculty at the Utah Valley State College Institute of Religion, where he serves as Director of Student Life. When asked to describe his personality, his wife says, "He is a teacher through and through: who is dedicated to serving others and making it fun! He loves being a husband and a dad!"

11

WILL YOU BE
THEIR FRIEND?

Randal A. Wright

Imagine for a moment that you meet two young men. Each is an outstanding fellow, and you are excited to be friends with both of them. After enjoying several months of good communication on deeply meaningful topics, they invite you to a reunion. Being a little shy, you ask how many will be at the reunion. When they say over 200 people will be in attendance, that seems a little frightening. In addition you learn that most of those who will be attending the reunion have been friends for years. The whole thing seems a little daunting, but you like your new friends so much you decide to accept their offer. They assure you that it will be a lot of fun and that you will soon be a part of their circle of friends. When you arrive at the site of the reunion your friends are waiting for you, lessening your fear. But approaching them, you hesitate a little, realizing that you won't know one person other than the two of them. As you approach the large group, a couple of people say hello as you walk by, but no one really talks to you. However, your friends are with you, so you feel reasonably comfortable. But after a very short time, your friends turn to you and say that they have to go now and that it was really nice getting to know you. When you ask where they are going, they tell you they are moving and will probably never see you again. Can they call you? No, they aren't allowed to call. But they assure you that the people at the reunion will take care of you and be your friends. Before you can even discuss it with them, they are gone, and you are left with a room full of strangers. What would you do at this point?

This imaginary scenario may help you understand how it must feel to new converts to the Church when they make their first attempt to attend meetings. After meeting the missionaries and hearing the gospel of Jesus Christ for the first time, the convert catches the vision of the joy that the gospel can bring into their lives. When the missionaries invite them to church, they may be leery of coming into a group of strangers in a foreign setting. From the convert's point of view, this new group resembles an established family, gathered in some kind of reunion. The members of the Church appear to know each other very well, and they share a camaraderie that is difficult to break into. To make matters worse, once the missionaries have brought them to church, the converts are on their own, especially when the elders are transferred, which they invariably are—often right away. Some of these converts are welcomed warmly and flourish. But, sadly, many are not cared for at all. Overall we are losing our new converts by the thousands worldwide. Unable to cope with being ignored or even rejected, they simply stay away. President Gordon B. Hinckley pleaded with bishops and Church members at the October 1997 general conference to be a friend to the new convert. He said:

"Someone has failed, failed miserably. I say to bishops throughout the world that with all you have to do— and we recognize that it is much—you cannot disregard the converts. Most of them do not need very much. As I have said before, they need a friend. They need something to do, a responsibility. They need nurturing with the good word of God. They come into the Church with enthusiasm for what they have found. We must immediately build on that enthusiasm. You have people in your wards who can be friends to every convert. They can listen to them, guide them, answer their questions, and be there to help in all circumstances and in all conditions. Brethren, this loss must stop. It is unnecessary. I am satisfied the Lord is not pleased with us. I invite you, every one of you, to make this a matter of priority in your administrative work. I invite every member to reach out in friendship and love for those who come into the Church as converts" (*Ensign,* November 1997, 51).

In summary, President Hinckley said our new converts need someone who will:

Be a friend

Give them something to do, a responsibility

Nurture them with the good word of God

Listen to them

Guide them

Answer their questions

Be there to help in all circumstances and in all conditions

Reach out in friendship and love.

As I sat in that conference and heard the words of our prophet, at first I thought, "Yes, we do have a problem. I sure hope the bishops take care of it!" Later, as I was reading President Hinckley's words from the conference report, the last sentence seemed to jump off the page at me. "*I invite every member to reach out in friendship and love for those who come into the Church as converts.*" I had to ask myself the question—how have I done in reaching out? The answer is not good. But I want to repent and do better. But how? As I searched for an answer to this question, I read a talk by Elder Carl B. Pratt of the Seventy, which he gave in that same conference. His talk was entitled "Care for New Converts," and he spoke of improving our "fellowshipping skills." I thought, *You know, I don't think I really know what it means to fellowship someone.* I pulled down the dictionary and looked under fellowshipping and read: "The condition or relation of belonging to the same class or group." In other words, when we fellowship new converts, we are to make them feel as if they belong to the same group as we do.

Have you ever known a convert who has fallen away from the Church? How did it happen? I wonder if we as members sometimes forget the commandment given by the Savior to "love thy neighbor as thyself" (Matthew 22:39). Consider the following situations.

NICHELLE

It is not easy to be the new person trying to break into established friendships. A few years ago our family made a major move to a new city. Our three girls left all their established friends and started a new school year, 1,300 miles away from their old friends. One of our daughters met a couple of girls at church and hoped to have the same lunch period at school with them, since that was the time of the school day that she feared most. One of the first days in school, she was sitting in the lunchroom eating by herself. She looked up to see one of the girls in our new ward walking toward her with a group of friends. As the girl neared the table where Nichelle was sitting, she started laughing and mockingly said, "You don't have any friends!" Then she turned around and walked away. That was a very hard day for our daughter. It is not fun to be on the outside when others are enjoying the company of friends. When this happens to new converts, often the result is that they just don't come back.

PAUL

Sometimes it's amazing how little effort it takes to fellowship someone if that fellowshipping comes from the right people. When I was teaching seminary, we had a student named Paul who came out a few times at the first of the year. However, he quit coming after a few weeks. During the year, his bishop and I tried several times to get him to come back, but without success. We essentially gave up trying until about two weeks before school was out that year. Then one day we had a lesson about reaching out to others.

This young man's name came up. I told the class that the bishop and I had tried all we knew to reach him and asked for their suggestions. Although everyone in the class really liked Paul, they all had their own friends and didn't really hang out with him. Someone suggested that every class member write him a note and tell him how they felt about him. They had some very nice things to say to Paul and sincerely expressed their desire to have him come back and be with us. The day after he got the messages, he came back to seminary for the first time in about eight months. He came every day after that until seminary ended for the summer. The following year, our friend never missed one day of seminary the entire year—even though the starting time was 5:55 A.M. This young man added an element of laughter and fun that would have been missed if he hadn't been there. Later, Paul served a mission and married in the temple. What had happened? The members of the class had simply reached out and made him feel comfortable and accepted. They drew him into their circle of friends.

RANDY

While serving in a youth leadership position, I had the opportunity to work with Caroline, who was one of our youth representatives. Caroline was asked to invite all the less actives to church, which she did. One of the people she contacted was Randy. Although he was a member, he hadn't been to church in years. She talked to him on the phone several times, but never actually met him. Finally, after Caroline had spent weeks inviting him to activities and church meetings, Randy agreed to come to a sacrament meeting. They arranged a meeting time and explained what they would be wearing, so they'd be able to recognize each other. When the meeting time arrived, Caroline looked all through the meetinghouse trying to find Randy, but she saw no one matching the description he had given her. She continued to look for him until after the meeting had started, but he was nowhere to be found. Fifteen minutes after the meeting started, she finally gave up and went in and sat down. When she got home, she called to ask why Randy had never shown up. He said that he had gotten to the church at their appointed time, but he couldn't find her. He had walked around the building until after the meeting started but finally gave up hope that she was going to meet him. It hit her that they had told each other what they would be wearing and the meeting time, but they did not discuss the exact meeting place. She assumed that they would meet inside the chapel and he assumed that she would be waiting outside for him. Caroline then asked Randy why he didn't just come into the building. He told her that he did not feel comfortable walking into a place filled with strangers.

And yet in the Church no one should feel like a stranger. "Ye are no more strangers and foreigners, but fellowcitizens with the saints, and of the household of God" (Ephesians 2:19). Imagine this young man walking around the building searching for a girl that he didn't even know, too self-conscious or timid to come in. I wonder how our converts feel when the missionaries baptize them and then get transferred, leaving them in the care of ward members. How are we doing in caring for new converts or those who are just coming back into church activity? Are we remembering the Savior's teaching, "A new commandment I give unto you, That ye love one another"? (John 13:34). Most of the time, it does not take much at all to make others feel welcome.

EUGENE

Several years ago my wife and I served as chairmen of a stake youth conference. Right before a scheduled planning meeting, my wife noticed Eugene, a recent convert to the Church. She describes what happened: "Out of the corner of my eye, I caught a glimpse of Eugene, a brand-new convert in our ward. He was small for his age, shy, and not too sure about his place in our large ward. I invited him into the meeting for those who would be attending youth conference. He told me that he wasn't planning to go to the youth conference. I assured him with a smile that he was going to go. At first he refused to go into the meeting. But he had that look in his eyes that said, 'I'd really like to be a part, I'm just a little scared.' So, I told him he'd love the meeting, linked my arm in his, and walked him into the room where the other youth and their parents had already assembled. He remained quiet throughout the meeting, but I could tell he was excited to be a part. A few weeks later Eugene was in attendance at Lamar University for our three-day youth conference. I have never seen anyone have as much fun and make as many new friends as Eugene did during those few days. The group completely accepted him and made him feel welcome. Several years after that, we were happy when Eugene accepted a mission call and later got married in the temple. He graduated from BYU and afterward earned a master's degree from the University of Texas. Today he is an active Church leader and very successful in his occupation. I guess some of us just need a little encouragement to become involved."

KINSEY

A few years ago, I moved with my family from Utah to Austin, Texas, to be the director of the institute of religion in the area. I had a lonely feeling as I walked into the institute building the first few days. One of the first people to greet me was Kinsey. She was a second year student at the University of Texas at Austin. She was very friendly and asked me about myself and my family. We talked for several minutes and then she told me that she was glad that we were there. This young lady was obviously a disciple of Christ. He said, "By this shall all men know that ye are my disciples, if ye have love one to another" (John 13:35). That welcome helped me feel much better about being in my new environment. From that point until now, she has gone out of her way to be friendly to me and my family. As I thought about this experience, I realized that Kinsey taught me a lot about how a newly arrived person should be treated. But she didn't reveal to me her own situation that day at the institute. You see, at the time Kinsey welcomed me to Austin, she was not a member of the Church. A few months later, however, she asked me to speak at her baptism. She had wanted to join the Church while she was in high school, but out of respect for her family's wishes, she waited until she got to college to be baptized. I asked her how she became interested in the Church. She wrote:

"I was not a member of the Church when I was in high school, but I started attending seminary when a friend in one of my school classes invited me to go. I met so many people in that seminary class and many of them helped me feel welcome. They introduced themselves, which meant a lot to me. It takes courage to go up to someone you don't know and try to get to know them. Many of the friends I made in that class didn't just introduce themselves once. They showed genuine continuing interest in me. The most important thing my friends in the Church did for me was invite me to do things with them. We did so many creative activities together, and we just had fun and got to know each other by hanging out. By spending time with me, they became my friends and not people I simply saw at church. One of my best friends looked for me when I came into church every Sunday by myself. As a youth, I felt a little out of place attending church alone since everyone else sat with their own families, and I did not have a family to sit with. My friend made sure I knew I could sit with his family. Another friend always found me after sacrament meeting and walked with me to Sunday School. That helped so much because I felt so different from all the other youth in the Church and even my friends. I knew I didn't understand as much about the gospel as they did because they had grown up with the Church and I hadn't. I felt inadequate to answer questions and felt somewhat like the 'black sheep.' By making real friends I felt more comfortable about being new. I think the biggest mistake we make in failing to retain new converts is thinking someone else is going to do it. We all need to be aware of new converts and do our part. One individual cannot do it all."

After Kinsey moved to Austin, she began attending church at the University Ward and coming to the activities at the institute. She continued what she had been taught by being a friend to others that came into the Church, even though she still had not joined herself. Consider the influence she had on Jennifer, also a university student and a new convert.

JENNIFER

"I'm thinking back to the time right after I was baptized to consider how I was able to understand all of the new things, accept a change in my life, and make friends in the Church. First of all, it is scary coming into a new place even if it is where you are supposed to be. So in pondering my situation and how I was able to stay active, several things come to mind.

"Kinsey comes to mind first. Even though she was not a member at the time, she came to my baptism (so many people came to my baptism). Scott (I don't remember his last name) introduced me to Kinsey. I don't think even today he fully understands what he did by bringing her to my baptism and introducing us. Soon after, Kinsey and I became best friends. She has helped me tremendously and was the one who introduced me to the Church sorority. Although there were only ten or so girls attending, they immediately took me in, and I joined the sorority. The sisterhood I received from them has made a huge difference throughout the past three years.

"The blessings of receiving callings was talked about during my discussions and after my baptism. I saw so many people continually working on their callings and having fun at it. So, naturally, when I received my first calling, I was very excited. I felt important; I felt like I had a part, a job to do, that somehow I was finally included in helping to make a difference.

"It is so hard to remember who did what because everyone did a lot. Whether they were going to parties, movies, or group activities, they always called me. You know what? They always called me!! Friends—to do things with. They came to me. Yes, I had to do my part, but they always called.

"I think it is very important to introduce converts to converts. We share a special bond with each other, especially in the beginning. We understand each others' perspectives. I got so much support and friendship from other recent converts like Matt, Jennifer, Courtney, and Cathy. And then there was Kinsey—although not yet a member, she was always there.

"There is something I have always felt bad about, however. Actually worse than bad. I was extremely blessed as a convert, but I forgot my role as a member. It is so important we remember our role in missionary and fellowship work. I remember Kara. She and I talked a lot. I felt like she was very open with me. We had a lot in common. But when she stopped coming to church, I did not do much. Did I care? Yes, I cared very much, but I was selfish and too wrapped up in my own life and desires. So I did very little. Could I have made a difference? I will never know because I never tried. So I ask myself and you: Are we friends with people only when it is convenient? Do we only befriend those who are 'our type,' or are we friends with people because we love them and are there to support them when they struggle? That, in my opinion, is the key to keeping our converts. We must be there for them."

Summarizing what converts Kinsey and Jennifer have said about what helped keep them strong and active in the Church, there were people who went out of their way to:
Introduce themselves
Continue approaching them in a friendly manner
Show genuine interest
Really care
Invite them to do things
Sit with them in church
Walk them to Sunday School class
Attend their baptism
Invite them to church functions

See to it that they became involved or received a calling

Invite them to social activities

Introduce them to other recent converts

Always be there.

Just an update on these two young women: Kinsey has been an Especially for Youth counselor and will graduate from the University of Texas this spring. Jennifer met an Especially for Youth counselor named Nathan at the Beaumont, Texas, session, where she was asked to sing at the counselor fireside. He had been scheduled to be in Massachusetts that week but had his assignment changed unexpectedly. They were married in the Dallas Temple on 27 December 1997. Our family will be forever grateful for Kinsey and others who helped a new convert named Jennifer feel accepted and loved. You see, Nathan, the EFY counselor she married, is our oldest son. Jennifer is now our daughter-in-law. You never know the future of the convert you will help fellowship.

We have been asked by a prophet of God to get out of our comfort zones and befriend new converts and others who may be struggling to feel accepted. The Lord spoke of this when he said, "For if ye love them which love you, what reward have ye? . . . And if ye salute your brethren only, what do ye more than others?" (Matthew 5:46–47). I challenge you, as I challenge myself, to go out of your way from this point forward to include the new convert in your life, regardless of their age.

Randal Wright comes from Austin, Texas, where he serves as the institute director for the Church Educational System. He has a Ph.D. in family studies from BYU. He has done extensive research on the impact of electronic media on adolescents. He has also written articles for several magazines and published four books. He and his wife, Wendy, have five children.

12

FORGIVE AND FORGET

Suzanne L. Hansen

Mike, a young teenager, was asked by his mother to put a large container of ice cream downstairs in the freezer. He was more than happy to do so. He rushed to complete the task and quickly moved on to another activity.

A couple of days later, Mike's mother made a momentous discovery!

In his "busyness," Mike had put the ice cream in the clothes dryer instead of the freezer. The dryer, right next to the freezer, had a completely different environment inside it—not exactly fit for ice cream.

Picture this. A melting "goo" oozing all over the inside and down into the workings of the dryer. In her shock, all Mike's mother could do was laugh. Despite the large repair bill and the inconvenience of not having a dryer for a few days, she determined not to dwell on the silly mistake. Her son was much more important than the ice cream, or even the dryer.

Because of his mother's forgiving attitude, Mike was very repentant and most anxious to do better. He had learned a lesson, although an expensive one: keep one's mind on what one is doing.

All of us have made some crazy or foolish mistakes in our lives. We may have even hurt another's feelings without trying to offend. Perhaps we've been the one offended. Then there are those who intentionally try to hurt others.

PICTURE THIS: BAD FEELINGS OOZING DOWN INSIDE US

You have probably heard someone say, "I'LL NEVER FORGIVE HIM FOR DOING THAT TO ME." Maybe you've also overheard someone else say, "I'll FORGIVE HER, BUT I'LL NEVER FORGET THIS FOR AS LONG AS I LIVE!"

The Savior had a strong rebuke for such. He said: "My disciples, in days of old, sought occasion against one another and forgave not one another in their hearts; and for this evil they were afflicted and sorely chastened" (D&C 64:8).

The Lord did not reveal how they were afflicted, but when one is troubled in their heart, there is no peace of mind, chaos rules, and serenity is lost. Jesus went on to say, "For he that forgiveth not his brother his trespasses standeth condemned before the Lord; for there remaineth in him the greater sin. I, the Lord, will forgive whom I will forgive, but of you it is required to forgive all men" (D&C 64:9–10).

True forgiveness, then, is a matter of HEART—a change of HEART. When we forgive someone their trespass, we are expected to truly forget the hurt, the bitterness, and let the matter go. Henry Ward Beecher once said, "To forgive and not to forget is really not to forgive."

How do you begin to forget an evil someone has done? I find it helps if I am able to look at the person who has hurt or offended me with my SPIRITUAL EYES. It makes a difference if you can see the person as a child of God who may be hurting or be fearful inside, to view their thoughtlessness or unkindness as perhaps the result of a troubled heart. Such behavior may be an attempt to get attention, and yes, even love. By looking at them with love and compassion rather than anger and judgment—and by praying sincerely that your heart will be softened—angry, bitter feelings will leave you; old grudges will crumble. Forgiving then will become more natural, and forgetting the hurt inside will be easier.

BE YOUR OWN DETECTIVE

Do you find it easy to forgive and forget? Try to get to know yourself and observe how you think, react to others, and live each day. Watch yourself to see where your thoughts are taking you. Be your own detective. Watch for CLUES that may reveal why you make the choices you do. You may begin to see things more clearly.

CLUE #1: Choosing Peace or Conflict Each Day?

Become aware of the number of times you get irritated in a day or the reasons people make you mad. Check the following list to see where you are:

a. Do you find yourself becoming impatient with teachers, slow drivers, a new store clerk, or someone who does not see things your way?

b. Is there a pattern to the things that make you lose your temper?

c. Do you find it consistently hard to get along with parents, family members, or friends?

d. Are you frequently unhappy and cross, without any real reason?

If you are having any of these reactions, maybe it's more than just a bad hair day or just another bad mood. Maybe you have an unforgiving heart.

Holding on to bad feelings and never resolving them can create a lot of turmoil inside. But truly forgiving can get you back on track.

HOW TO FORGIVE AND FORGET THE HURT

When I really started to watch my own actions and reactions to people throughout the day, I was surprised and sometimes shocked by how unforgiving and judgmental I could be. This process of truly forgiving others is difficult. I knew I needed to forgive, and then forget, but how to do it? I spent time reading and learning about the subject.

I ran across a book in which Dr. Gerald Jampolsky, a medical doctor, suggests that we remind ourselves daily to let go of the past and get over the fear of the future—to live in the present moment. Right NOW you can choose to start forgiving. It doesn't matter how many times we relive in our minds something that happened, we can't change it. We can only take the lesson taught by each situation we encounter, and move forward.

CLUE #2: Take a Leap of Faith and Trust in God.

Trusting that God loves us completely and eternally, and that the power of his love is always with us, can give us the courage to move forward, moment by moment. It is knowing that we can trust his strength rather than our own limited, meager supply. Knowing this makes it easier to forgive. God knows all. He knows what is best for us. We just have to trust that.

In his book, Dr. Jampolsky tells the story of Derek Schmidt, a ten-year-old boy who had leukemia. When his cancer went into remission, Derek's parents were understandably relieved and praised God for being mindful of their son. But when the disease suddenly reappeared, they lost faith.

We can understand that, can't we? It is difficult to trust God when we think our prayers have gone unanswered, and these good people complained bitterly to Dr. Jampolsky that they felt alone and forsaken.

Derek taught his parents a great lesson, and Dr. Jampolsky wept as the afflicted young boy said: "You don't have to understand everything to have faith and trust in God, all we have to know is that God loves us, all the time, and that nothing ever happens to us that we cannot handle with His help" (*Good Bye to Guilt* [1985], 64).

To me, this boy was a wise soul in a very young body, reminding all of us what faith and trust in God is all about.

CLUE #3: Choose to Be a Love-Giver.

There are perhaps two kinds of people: love-givers and love-seekers. Love-givers give just for the joy of giving. Love-seekers are those who need love and attention and will do almost anything to get it. Because love-seekers are often frustrated, they can come across as mean or unkind. The "show-off" is often really asking for love and attention. However, our first reaction may be to ignore such people and make a judgment about them that sticks with us.

While driving along Redwood Road in Salt Lake City one day, I pulled up to a stoplight behind a station wagon with three young children in the back. Before we pulled ahead, all three kids flipped me the bird. At first, I was upset. But then I realized that I could choose how to react. I could get angry and pull the parents over to tell them what rotten children they had. I could scowl at the children and wag my finger at them. Or . . . I could forgive them and send an indication of love to the children. I chose the latter.

I smiled and waved, and they promptly waved back, with smiles on their faces. Traffic started to move forward, and as we traveled along together for the next few blocks, the children continued to smile and wave enthusiastically until out of sight. Instead of making three enemies, I had just made three friends. I may not have spoken to them, but I gave them an "I-love-you-you're-important" message just the same; and they responded.

As I continued driving, enjoying my forgiving spirit, I realized that the children probably didn't even know what they were doing. No doubt, they had seen others flip people off, and when they tried it, they got a reaction. Monkey see, monkey do. They were not bad children. They were just children needing attention.

FORGIVE EVERYONE!

There is an old song that says, "You always hurt the one you love, the one you shouldn't hurt at all." And it's true, those who love each other most and who ought to be most thoughtful of each other often inflict the greatest wounds. It's ironic, too, that in a way, it's much easier to forgive perfect strangers than it is to forgive those we know and love when *they* offend us. The list of those needing our forgiveness and love could start with parents, brothers, sisters, and other family members. (And what about Aunt Bessie? Have you forgiven her yet for embarrassing you at the family reunion?)

Since you're making out your list, what about your bossy or unkind neighbors, Church members, teachers, leaders, employers, teammates, and even world leaders who may have caused suffering? If we want to be happy, we must examine our hearts to see what bitterness we might be storing there and do something to get rid of it.

Remember, the Lord will forgive whom he will forgive, but we are required to forgive . . . and love . . . EVERYONE (see D&C 64: 8–10).

Loving everyone doesn't mean that we have to invite them over for a barbecue or even send a Christmas present. Love usually indicates the absence of hate. Hate and bitterness are what canker the soul. By being forgiving and charitable, we can keep this important commandment. When it comes to dealing with people and their faults and shortcomings, I have found we can love them best by developing total amnesia. Just forget it.

"Okay," you say. "But what if someone keeps doing the same thing over and over to hurt or bug you? How do you handle that? How often am I required to forgive?"

When Jesus was asked this question, he said we should forgive seventy times seven for the same offense (see Matthew 18:21–22). Literally, that would be 490 times! Obviously, the Savior meant there should be no limit to our willingness to forgive those who offend us.

CLUE #4: Cleansing the Heart of Old Hurts.

A friend of mine, I'll call him Dale, told me of the bad feelings he had held all his life toward his father. Now an older man, Dale still had a hard time being with his father, for the old feelings would come up. Finally, as his father lay dying in a hospital, Dale knew he must do something, but how could he face his father, and speak the words, "I forgive you"? How could he truly let go of the memory of all the cruel and unjust things that his father had done to him?

Dale remembered the scripture where the Savior says we must forgive seventy times seven times. He decided to write down those things his father had done that had hurt him so, and then before each offense he would write, "I forgive my father for . . . "

He wrote each forgiveness 490 times. It took him hours—most of the night. As he finally completed his self-appointed task, the anger seemed to leave, and he began to feel a loving, forgiving spirit. His stony heart had truly changed. The blame was gone, and he was filled with love and compassion for his father.

He felt such peace that he called each of his brothers and sister and suggested that they do the same. Each of them, in turn, experienced this same healing, and they decided to hold a prayer circle around their father's deathbed in the hospital. After the prayer, they each forgave him and asked for his forgiveness. Dale said there was a great sense of peace in the room. Their father had been lingering for weeks, but after this special experience, he quietly and peacefully passed away. It was as though he had been waiting for that moment.

CLUE #5: Forgiving When It Seems Impossible to Forgive.

Forgiving an unkind word or act, even when we have been offended over and over again, is one thing. But what if someone has done something unthinkable and abhorrent? How could you ever forgive someone who kills one of your family members? This happened to Zalinda Dorcheous.

In August of 1970, her second son, John, was murdered. He was only twenty years old. The brutal and senseless act sent a shock wave of grief and bitterness through the whole community. But no one was more hateful than Zalinda.

The man who killed John was tried, convicted, and sent to prison. After a few years, he came up for parole. Zalinda was at the hearing with her family and friends, giving emotional testimony of the irreparable damage this man had done. His parole was denied. She made it her mission to keep him behind bars—in doing so, she continually fanned the fires of her hatred and resentment.

Every time he became eligible for parole, she showed up to regurgitate all her bitterness. Zalinda felt that her emotions and behavior were both normal and appropriate. After all, the man had robbed her of her son. How else should she feel?

But Zalinda had no peace of mind. Her health and other relationships were suffering. She began to question the value of her life.

Then Zalinda took a bold step. She enrolled in a class on how to heal one's attitude and life. She began to look at things differently and knew her hatred was hurting her the most. She knew she had to forgive.

Zalinda wrote to the man in prison and asked to meet with him. I'm sure he was as apprehensive as she was. This woman was his enemy. She was the principal reason that he had been denied parole, hearing after hearing. Imagine how stiff and awkward that first meeting was, the only time she had ever spoken to him face to face. It was very difficult for her to address him by his first time, Michael, instead of calling him that miserable "so and so."

As Zalinda continued to visit Michael in prison, she slowly began letting go of the old images of him that she had been carrying. She began to see him in the present, without his past. Before her was emerging a human being with fears as well as hopes—an insecure person with talents and potential—not a wicked monster.

Zalinda then made this observation, "I do not understand myself what is happening, I only know I am doing what I have to do, and it feels good. I have had enough of pain and anger. More and more I can feel myself coming from a heart filled with peace and love. It feels really good, and I love it!"

Somewhere in this process, Zalinda forgave the man who took her son's life. Now she was able to put her energy into helping him rather than hating him.

At Michael's last parole hearing, Zalinda spoke on his behalf. It was because of her testimony that Michael was released on 17 July 1989. On that momentous day, Zalinda herself was there in her car to pick him up. There was also a job waiting for him.

Shortly after Michael was released from prison, *The Today Show* did a feature on Zalinda and Michael, generating an overwhelming emotional response. People were moved by the story and several offers even came from well-known movie studios to do Zalinda's and Michael's story (see Gerald Jampolsky, *One Person Can Make a Difference* [1990], 13–28).

As I read about Zalinda's experience, I kept asking myself, *If my son were murdered, would I really be able to forgive his killer?* I hope so because I know the Lord would require it of me.

CLUE #6: Love the World.

When the Savior said that we were to become as little children (see Matthew 18:3), one of the things he might have had in mind was that we would view the world without prejudice and bias. Children are quick to love and quick to forgive. Only later in life do they learn prejudice, usually from adults.

Some years ago, a boy named Bill lived in a small town in Florida. He heard that the Russians were our enemies. He began to wonder about the Russian children and could not believe that they could be his enemies, too. He decided to do something about it and wrote a short letter:

> *Dear Comrade in Russia:*
> *I am writing to a six-year-old friend in Russia.*
> *I am seven years old, and I believe that we can*

*live in peace. I want to be your friend, not your
enemy. Will you become my friend and write to me?
Love and Peace, Bill*

He then folded his note, put it neatly into an empty bottle, and threw the bottle into what he thought was the ocean. Well, the "ocean" happened to be an inland lake, and about five days later someone found the bottle with the note in it, only about seventy yards from where Bill had stood on the beach and thrown it into the water.

When an article about Bill's note appeared in the local newspaper, Bill and his parents came forward to claim the letter and were interviewed. The Associated Press picked up the story, and pretty soon the account was being published all around the world. A group of people from New Hampshire, who were taking children to the Soviet Union as ambassadors of peace, read the article. They contacted Bill and invited him to come to the Soviet Union with them. The little boy became a wonderful peacemaker (see Jampolsky, *One Person Can Make a Difference*, 196–97).

I love the innocence that is at the heart of that story. Bill had very little past experience to interfere with his thoughts about what might be possible. He decided that he could make a difference, and he acted on that. For me, this story demonstrates that when a heart is pure, nothing is impossible. It also gives life to the biblical saying, "A little child shall lead them" (Isaiah 11:6).

Jesus gave a new commandment. He said, "Love one another; as I have loved you"(John 13:34).

FORGIVING OURSELVES IS THE BEGINNING OF LOVE

Mother Teresa taught, "Once you know you have hurt someone, be the first to say sorry. We cannot forgive unless we know that we need forgiveness, and forgiveness is the beginning of love" (*The Joy in Loving* [1996], 78).

Now here is probably the most important point.

The Savior said that we should love our neighbors as ourselves. If forgiveness is the beginning of love, as

Mother Teresa states, then we must first forgive ourselves before we can begin to forgive and truly love others. Let go of your mistakes. Don't dwell on your blunders. Love yourself enough to forgive yourself. And then, seek forgiveness from others. Finally, enjoy the soothing balm of peace that can come from the Savior when you seek his forgiveness.

The experience of writing this chapter has been wonderful. I have recalled the times when I have felt a sweet serenity wash over my heart and soul. It has come through forgiving and forgetting. I hope you too can experience firsthand the peace that awaits you.

Suzanne Hansen was born in San Francisco, California, and is married to Michael D. Hansen. They are proud parents of three children: Jenny, John, and Julie. Suzanne is the author of five books and three tape programs. She was Honor Mother for the state of Utah in 1980, has served in the Young Women organization for much of the last twenty years.

13

THE DESIRES
OF OUR HEART

Vickey Pahnke

Desire is the pilot of the soul." Elder Sterling W. Sill said this at a BYU address in 1965. It is from our *desires* that our thoughts, words, and actions spring. They *drive* us, so to speak. It has occurred to me that if we can better align our desires, we will find ourselves flying first class through this mortal journey rather than sitting in the economy section of life.

What are your desires? How do you *feel* about things? Where is your heart? Anyone reading this chapter who wants to lose weight, stand up. Or, if you wish you were taller or shorter or smarter or that you had better teeth or that your ears didn't flap in the breeze, take a number and join a BIG club. *Everyone* seems to be dissatisfied with some aspect of their physical self. We compare and contrast and moan and quietly mumble at something, some time or another. There are things we are able to improve— if we have the *desire*. We may be able to gain or lose weight, grow our hair or color it, even go under a plastic surgeon's knife to change our appearance. If the desire is strong enough, we will commit to do what it takes. There are other things that cannot be changed. If our desire is to be satisfied with our physical selves, then we will be happier . . . kind of like moving up a row or two on the plane.

Similarly, once we have a desire to improve our personality and our spiritual tone, we are freed up to *act* on that desire. We will commit to do what is required, only if we truly have the desire to do so. It sometimes takes no more than a personal belief in our ability to exercise and change our eating habits to change the shape of our bodies. In order to make a difference, we must "wake up and smell the roses" and implement a health plan.

The same principle applies in our quest for spiritual development and improvement! "But behold, if ye will awake and arouse your faculties, even to an experiment upon my words, and exercise a particle of faith, yea, even if ye can no more than desire to believe, let this desire work in you, even until ye believe in a manner that ye can give place for a portion of my words" (Alma 32:27). Hey! those words "awake," "experiment," and "exercise" are *action* words, based on *desire*. Even if we can't change the shape of our physical bodies, we can certainly enhance the shape of our spiritual selves.

This quote from Elder Neal A. Maxwell is food for thought: "What we insistently desire, over time, is what we will eventually become and what we will receive in eternity" (*Ensign,* November 1996, 21). My hope and prayer for you, my young friend, is for your eternal happiness. The journey to forever is in progress. Can we trim our desires for worldly, useless things in order to focus our desires on the things that will make us forever joyful? Let's address four things that may affect our desires for good:

THE IMPORTANCE OF PERSONAL ACCOUNTABILITY

We must desire to be **PERSONALLY ACCOUNTABLE.** Too often we place the blame on another for our own shortcomings or mistakes. Society many times excuses criminal activity, blaming the environment, the family, or some pitiful circumstance for a person's willful act. What has happened? Even in our more secure gospel setting, it is becoming more prevalent to point the finger of blame at someone else rather than take a gulp and admit, "It was my fault." Doesn't it make sense that if we are willing to be responsible for our own thoughts and actions, we will more carefully measure them? DESIRE to be personally responsible for your life's work and worth. The Lord will judge us mercifully and lovingly, but he will not accept excuses for us not reaching our potential because _____ (you fill in the blank here). It is the adversary who would have us believe that because something unfair or harmful has happened to us, we are excused from moving positively and productively forward! If you have a homework assignment, turn it in. If you didn't do it, *say* you didn't do it. If you are in a bad mood, take the responsibility to change your mood—without blaming it on your family or boy/girlfriend. Come unto Christ and be a good Christian, regardless of circumstances. No more excuses!

WE MUST DESIRE TO SUCCEED

Elder Hartman Rector Jr. said that "If the desire is strong enough, performance is assured" (*Ensign,* May 1979, 29). This means that if you do your best, you will experience success. Not as a neighbor experiences success, perhaps, but you'll enjoy the success right for *you.* You might want to spend some time defining your idea of success and then make sure it is in keeping with the Lord's ideas. Then go for it! Don't let anyone tell you that you can't do something.

While a student at BYU (this was back in the Stone Age), I studied musical theater and was part of a theater company. All my life, I had been known as the "harmony girl."

When only three, I had the ability to hear harmony lines and sing them and that was what I was comfortable doing. While performing, I always stayed safely within the bounds of my "assigned" place. Solos were out for me because it had always been my place to sing alto or second soprano or whatever was needed to assist the lead singer.

Then one day we learned that there would be some changes in the company and a new lead would be needed. I can still vividly remember the experience of standing on the stage as the director moved down the line of cast members. When he stood in front of one of us, it was an invitation to that person to audition for the lead spot. Even though my heart was pounding and my hands were sweating, I had decided it was time to go for it. I was determined to step forward and give it my best shot.

The tall fellow standing ahead of me was a great guy and extremely talented. Everyone looked up to him and he was highly respected. Probably in an effort to be helpful, he said to the director, "Oh, Vickey doesn't sing lead—she's our harmony person!"

I froze in my place with an embarrassed grin on my face and watched the director move on.

I thought, *I don't sing lead . . . only harmony.* It wasn't my castmate's fault. He was a good guy who had no intention of hurting my feelings or holding me back. And *he* didn't hold me back . . . *I* did. For a while, I blamed him for making me miss out. But if my *desire* had been strong enough, and if I had had enough intestinal fortitude, I would have gone for it.

Don't allow someone else's actions—however innocent—to keep you from progressing. If your desires (there is that word again!) are good and your goals worthy, you CAN succeed. You can go forward, even in a backward world. "Shall we not go on in so great a cause? Go forward and not backward" (D&C 128:22). What greater cause can there be than the assurance of our own salvation and helping in the Lord's work? If you desire to be better and do better, you will succeed in those efforts. Whether as a football player, a dancer, an artist, a friend, or whatever, work to succeed.

WE MUST BE COURAGEOUS

An actress named Tallulah Bankhead once said, "Nobody can be exactly like me. Sometimes even I have trouble doing it." Perhaps we should desire **COURAGE**. Courage to learn who we are and to be that person all the time—"at home, at school, at play" (I still love that Primary song about being a "sunbeam" for Jesus). You need to have the courage to be unashamed "to take upon you the name of Christ" (Mormon 8:38). Even when it is very hard to do so.

There were these three Jewish guys who were good friends and good followers of the Lord. The head of the community told them to knock it off with the worship thing and to do what everybody else was doing. He told them that if they continued to be sanctimonious (holier-than-thou), they were going to feel the heat. Literally. The names of the three are Shadrach, Meshach, and Abed-nego. The "leader's" name is King Nebuchadnezzar. If you will turn in your Old Testament to the third chapter of Daniel, and if you will ask for the Spirit's help, you will *feel* of Shadrach, Meshach, and Abed-nego's courage. Their courage was immediately rewarded, for they came out of the fiery furnace without a hair on their heads being singed or even the smell of smoke on them (see Daniel 3:12–30).

Abinadi is another scriptural friend who exemplified courage. In the 17th chapter of Mosiah, we learn the tragic end of a valiant mortal life. Abinadi had the courage of his convictions and the desire to be in the service of the Lord. For his faithful efforts, he ended up being burned at the stake.

At your school or in your community, maybe even in your own family, you might feel very alone. You might be ridiculed for your desires to be good: "Just once won't hurt!" "Don't be a geek, everybody else is doing it." "Why do you have to go to church *every* Sunday?" Hang in there and do what your heart tells you is right. As you go through your own "furnace of affliction" with courage, all will be well. Abinadi is just fine now, thank you. If, as it was with Abinadi, your good efforts are not being imme-diately rewarded, find peace, my young friend. Your courage will pay great dividends when you come face to face with the One who has it in his power to reward you eternally.

THE IMPORTANCE OF LOVE

There is an old tune entitled, "Love Makes the World Go 'Round." Indeed, just as when taking a ride on a merry-go-round, we may feel "up" or "down" or as though we're going in circles as a result of our loving or difficult relationships. When we feel we are loved, our journey is SO much better. Maybe not easier, but definitely better. Bishop H. Burke Peterson shared this profound thought: "Impossible mountains are climbed by those who have the self-confidence that comes from truly being loved. Prisons and other institutions, even some of our own homes, are filled with those who have been starved for affection" (*Ensign,* May 1977, 69). Perhaps we need to pray for the desire to **LOVE**. Not the desire *for* love, but the desire *to* love. Once we begin to really understand Christlike love, our whole understanding of life and its purpose increases. Pray, work for, *desire* to "love the Lord thy God with all thy heart" (D&C 59:6). His love allows us to have more love for everyone else . . . even the teacher whose class we suffer through or our little brother who drives us crazy sometimes. The author of the following poem is unknown. I imagine that you, as I, will wish you could personally thank the poet for this thought:

> *I ASKED GOD*
>
> *I asked God to take away my pride,*
> *And God said, "No."*
> *He said that it was not for Him to take away,*
> *But for me to give up.*
> *I asked God to make my handicapped child whole,*
> *And God said, "No."*
> *He said her spirit is whole;*
> *Her body is only temporary.*
> *I asked God to grant me patience,*

And God said, "No."
He said that patience is a by-product of tribulation—
It isn't granted, it's earned.
I asked God to give me happiness,
And God said, "No."
He said he gives us blessings—
Happiness is up to me.
I asked God to spare me pain,
And God said, "No."
He said suffering draws you apart from worldly cares
And brings you closer to Me.
I asked God if He loves me,
And God said, "Yes."
He gave His only Son who died for me,
And I will be in heaven someday
Because I believe.
I asked God to help me love others
As much as He loves me,
And God said,
"Ah, my child, now you understand."

The world is starving for want of affection, and Christ offers a banquet of love! You can be an instrument in his loving hands to make others feel noticed, needed, noble. The pure love of Christ or charity (see Moroni 7:47) diminishes our need for personal recognition or immediate, worldly rewards. We can sincerely congratulate the girl who made the cheerleading squad, even though we missed out. Or be glad for the friend who scores twenty points per basketball game. We can find satisfaction in doing for others, even if no one ever finds out. The One who loves us most *is* aware that our hearts are in the right place . . . and loves us for our efforts. Thank you, dear friends, for having righteous desires. Thanks to people like the students of Murray High School in Utah who elected a mentally handicapped girl to be their homecoming queen. How inspiring is the love they showed for a beautiful young lady who many may have considered the least likely candidate for such an office!

I believe this chapter is for you—the one who *wants* to be more committed to quality travel. The one who needs only a small suggestion or two to make a big difference in his or her flight pattern. The winners in life's journey will not be those who have accumulated the greatest number of things or who have most successfully hidden their mistakes. Rather, it will be those who have learned to depend on the Savior to direct their paths through the troubles and pitfalls. He loves us with his whole heart. If you wish to succeed, give to him the desires of *your* heart. You will work harder at proper accountability. You will enjoy real, substantial success as a person. Your courage will be increased. Your capacity to love will deepen and intensify. And yours will be the privilege of one day being piloted back to the place where he waits to take us in his loving arms.

Vickey Pahnke studied at BYU and gained bachelor's and master's degrees in communication. She works as a songwriter, vocalist, and producer. Vickey and her husband, Bob, are the parents of four children. She has spoken for BYU Education Week, Know Your Religion, EFY, and Outreach youth programs. She loves mountains, laughter, kids of all ages, music, food, teaching, cooking, and traveling. But mostly, she loves being a mom.

14

"ENGRAVEN UPON YOUR COUNTENANCE"

Lisa H. Olsen

My two-year-old son, Cole, thinks he's a dog. Brent, my husband, and I eagerly await his morning ritual of waking up. We hear a few kicks on the crib, a few spins of the dial on his crib toy, and then it happens. "ARF! ARF!" The barking begins. This has happened every morning for the past six months. He barks and barks until we come. If he thinks we are slow to respond, the barking becomes more intense.

We think it started because every morning our neighborhood is full of barking dogs. It is the first thing Cole hears when he awakens, so it is easy for him to think that is the way people wake up too. Our sweet little impressionable boy mimics everything.

Cole also mirrors my behavior. He loves to put on makeup with me in the morning. As a newborn he would sit in his car seat and watch me. When his chubby little fingers were able to hold things, he would pull the makeup away from me and try to open it. Now that his dexterity has developed, he not only can open all the containers, but he can also put the contents on his face. The funniest application is of a deep maroon eye shadow. He takes the wand, wets it in the corner of his tiny mouth, and pulls it up the side of his cheek to his eye, dragging a maroon line along its path. By the time he's done, he looks as if he has camouflaged his face for war. I laugh at the results. He wants to be like his mommy.

Cole mimics his father, too. Brent is an avid reader. When Cole sees him reading, he runs to his books, chooses one, turns the pages, and starts to mumble out loud. When he wants Brent's attention, he finds a tool catalog out of the magazine basket, wiggles his way into Brent's lap, and opens the magazine. "Was dat?" he asks. Brent replies with a technical name of the tool and Cole does his best to say it back. Cole loves tools because he watches his dad study the catalog and sees him use the tools often. He wants to be like his dad.

Have you ever admired someone so much that you tried to be like them? I find that it is particularly true for teenagers who are establishing their own identity and personality. I challenge you to carefully choose your examples, your heroes, your role models, and decide if they are worthy of your admiration. As baptized members of the Church we have taken upon us the name of Christ and have covenanted to stand as witnesses of God (see Mosiah 18:9). It would seem logical that after making such a serious commitment, we would look up to people who also follow Christ's example.

Everyone knows "situational" Mormons, those who change themselves to fit each situation in life. One time they are serious about the gospel, the next moment it's not clear where they stand. Alma speaks to these people, the baptized members of the Church, in the Book of Mormon version of general conference. If you ever wonder if your life is in harmony with the gospel, ask yourself all the questions Alma poses. In Alma 5:14 he asks, "And now behold, I ask of you, my brethren of the church, have ye spiritually been born of God? Have ye received his image in your countenances? Have ye experienced this mighty change in your hearts?"

When people look at you, do they see the Savior's

teachings reflected in your face and in your eyes? Before my mission I had heard of other missionaries who were stopped by people and asked, "What's different about you?" or told, "There's something in your eyes." Then it happened to me. Around Christmastime in a very cold Dijon, France, my companion and I knocked on the door of Jean-Pierre, who had once studied to be a Catholic priest. He knew exactly who we were, and he was very kind to us. He looked into our eyes and simply uttered, "You have a light in your eyes—that tells me that you believe in what you are doing!" I was stunned. The fact that Jean-Pierre used the word *light* amazed me even more. "The light of the body is the eye: if therefore thine eye be single, thy whole body shall be full of light" (Matthew 6:22). The word *light* means even more to me as I think of all the references to the Savior as the Light. Christ is the light in the darkness (see D&C 6:21). He is the true light which is in man (see D&C 88:50). Jean-Pierre saw the Savior's light shining in my countenance. Oh, how I would love always to have that compliment.

Alma continues the thought of reflecting the Savior's countenance a little later when he asks, "I say unto you, can ye look up to God at that day with a pure heart and clean hands? I say unto you, can you look up, having the image of God engraven upon your countenances?" (Alma 5:19). There is a subtle difference. One tiny word is almost missed but is packed with significance: *engraven.* The image of God **engraven** upon your countenance.

Two years ago, while reading this passage of scripture, I made a connection with a lesson I was teaching my art students about printmaking processes. Engraving is one of these processes. A metal plate, zinc or copper, is covered with a thick brown acid resist. The artist uses a sharp tool to scratch a contour line drawing of his subject. This exposes the metal of the plate in a tiny, thin, beautiful line. The plate is then placed into a bath of nitric acid for only three to five minutes. This is enough time for the acid literally to eat a groove into the plate only where the metal has been exposed. Once the line is etched into the plate by the acid, it can never be changed. It is a permanent marking. Alma asks if the image of Christ and God is etched so deeply into our countenances that it is permanent. If the image remains, regardless of the things we go through. When we receive Christ's image in our countenance, we should strive to become permanently committed to follow the example of the Savior's perfect life. Our commitment should never change, regardless of our situations in life.

I admire people who have overcome adversity or sin to follow the Savior and receive his image. Many go through the process of repentance to receive his image. My sister Nancy met such a man while serving a mission in Canada. She and her companion met James in the Salvation Army halfway house. Nancy said he was the scariest looking man in the lobby. He was dressed completely in black, covered with tattoos, and had nicotine-stained fingers, fingernails, and teeth. It was obvious that he cared little about his appearance. He had been in prison where he had seen a "Mormon" commercial on TV and had begged the guards for a Book of Mormon. Nobody would bring him one. During his seventeen years in prison, James never once slept all the way through the night, a victim of haunting dreams of the Vietnam War. Upon his release, James contacted the missionaries. They taught him the first discussion, and he loved it. When they gave him his own copy of the Book of Mormon, he held it tight, amazed that he finally had his own.

That night he read his first passages of scripture. Early the next morning, he eagerly reported that the previous night was the first time in seventeen years that he had slept through the night without a nightmare. He was convinced it was the result of reading scripture. The missionaries continued to teach James, always with the assistance of other ward members. Nancy noticed that the more he learned about the gospel and Christ, the more James changed his physical appearance and even his countenance. He started to wear nicer and cleaner clothes, and he shaved and cleaned up his face. As the lessons went on, James developed the feeling that he needed to repent. He began the serious process of not only conversion but repentance. The atonement of the Savior was real to him. After a time, James was challenged to be baptized. He accepted without hesitation and set a date. Because he had been in prison, he was required to be interviewed by the mission president.

The morning of the interview he discovered that all four of his tires had been slashed. He knew he had to get to the interview but didn't know anyone with a car. James ran and walked for three hours to get to his interview. He was found worthy to be baptized.

One of the last times my sister saw James was the evening of his baptism. His entire appearance had changed. As she spoke at the short service, he sat before her dressed in white, clean shaven, hair cut, and worthy. He didn't even look like the same person. Because he had chosen to follow the example of the Savior, everything had changed for him. The image of God and the image of Christ were beginning to be permanently engraved in his countenance.

There is a similar story in the scriptures of a young man who overcame adversity and sin to follow the Savior. Alma the Younger had been a troubled youth. He was described as "a very wicked and an idolatrous man. And he was a man of many words, and did speak much flattery to the people; therefore he led many of the people to do after the manner of his iniquities. And he became a great hinderment to the prosperity of the church of God" (Mosiah 27:8–9). Not a very positive description, is it? One day he was out with the sons of Mosiah, continuing to try to pull people away from the Church. While they were on their path of destruction, they received a surprise visit from an angel. Young Alma's father, Alma the prophet, had been praying that his misguided son might "be brought to the knowledge of the truth" (Mosiah 27:14). Alma and the sons of Mosiah fell to the earth because they were "astonished" (that's an understatement). The angel asked them why they persisted in persecuting the church of God. They didn't have an answer. The angel commanded them to cease their efforts to destroy the Church. Alma was so overwhelmed that he fell again to the earth and could not speak (v. 19). His friends carried their helpless friend to his father. Alma rejoiced because his son was dumb, for he recognized the power of God. When Alma the younger could finally speak he said, "Behold I am born of the Spirit. . . . My soul hath been redeemed from the gall of bitterness and bonds of iniquity. I was in the darkest abyss; but now I behold the marvelous light of God. My soul was racked with eternal torment; but I am snatched, and my soul is pained no more" (Mosiah 27:24, 29).

Alma the Younger became a committed and effective missionary, devoting years of his life to his ministry. He felt the power of the Atonement in his life and was compelled to share his testimony with others. "Now they were desirous that salvation should be declared to every creature, for they could not bear that any human soul should perish; yea, even the very thoughts that any soul should endure endless torment did cause them to quake and tremble" (Mosiah 28:3).

These experiences helped prepare Alma to be the first chief judge of the people of Nephi. When Nehor, an anti-Christ, came among them, many of the Nephite members were excommunicated or became inactive. The faithful members of the Church were tried. "Now this was a great trial to those that did stand fast in the faith; nevertheless, they were steadfast and immovable in keeping the commandments of God, and they bore with patience the persecution which was heaped upon them" (Alma 1:25). I love the word *HEAPED.* They didn't receive just a few trials, but instead it rained and poured trials. Do you ever feel as though you are heaped upon with trials? At those times, does the image of God still shine through?

My friend Karen had more physical trials heaped on her than any person I have met. But the image of God was engraven on her countenance. We first met in elementary school when I moved to Utah from California. Karen was smart, funny, and had a lot of friends. She also had the best birthday parties of any friend. As a child she nourished a deep and mature faith in God. When she was only twelve she wrote this in her journal: "As I went to bed and was saying my prayers, I was asking Heavenly Father how I could become a real good person. Suddenly I thought of the line from *Saturday's Warrior*— 'Your problem is you want all the answers at once.' That was it, do one little thing at a time and don't lose your faith and you'll succeed. I thanked God for helping me and climbed into bed" (Gladys Clark Farmer, *Karen's Test* [1989], 127). Our friendship continued through high school. She was like any other teenager at Timpview until her sophomore year when doctors discovered a rare form of neurofibromatosis (the Elephant Man's disease). Karen had the worst form possible—multiple internal tumors. Over a period of three years, Karen had six major surgeries to remove tumors or to correct the effects of the previous surgeries. She wrote in her journal, "Moreover, during the surgery, nerves were damaged, which caused complete deafness in my right ear, paralysis on the right side of my face, and paralysis of my vocal cords. I lost much of my balance, walked with difficulty, could not run, spoke only in whispers, had sight and hearing impairments, and could not smile. Half a year after this surgery, I was ready to resume the carefree lifestyle of a teenager, but I soon found that normal life would elude me forever" (*Karen's Test*, 50).

Karen had to communicate by writing on a clipboard or through a newly acquired skill of sign language. Her deafness caused tremendous loneliness because people began to avoid her, not knowing how to communicate. Because of the paralysis of her vocal cords, she had difficulty swallowing, and she had a plastic feeding tube inserted into her stomach. Each day she would go through the tedious process of putting baby formula down the tube.

I knew Karen during all those years and never once heard her complain. She patiently listened to my struggles, my heartaches, and was always compassionate and caring. I never really understood the extent of her suffering until I read her personal journal entries in a book about her life. It was her faith in God, the image that was engraven on her countenance, that pulled her through.

Just before I left to serve my mission, Karen bore her testimony in our young adult ward. She never seemed to miss church, even though it was difficult for her to understand the speakers. She pulled her frail body up to the podium and simply said that sometimes she wished she would have had the *luxury* (I never forgot that word) of worrying about the things we worry about. She then named some of the things that she had so patiently listened to us complain about. But then she surprised us by stating that she was amazed that we could get through the things we did. She thanked God for her physical trials because as a result she had never had to worry about breaking the Word of Wisdom or the law of chastity. She had gained a testimony that her afflictions had brought her closer to and made her more like Christ.

Karen died a month before I came home from my mission. She wished she could have served a mission like so many of her friends, and for one short month, our missions—mine on earth and hers in the spirit world—overlapped. On her funeral program was printed a poem she wrote, which is also her testimony:

TRUST ME

He'd said to trust Him,
To just keep following and trust Him.
We wandered on and on.
Sometimes we were in beautiful meadows of clover,
Or lush green forests,
Or dazzling canyons.
But other times we traveled through infested swamps
Or scorching deserts.
These times were almost more than I could bear,
And I often had to remind myself

I must keep following.
But then we reached a towering mountain,
So tall I could barely see the top.
He started straight up the steep pathway
With me following,
One step, then another.
How could I take any more?
"Can't we stop?" I screamed.
Oh, how I wanted to just quit—
To fall to the earth
And let myself roll back down the mountain.
He said nothing, but just continued on
With me somehow following.
Up and up and up we climbed,
Finally reaching the top.
I stumbled more than walked down the other side of the
mountain,
But reaching the bottom,
I saw we were in the most beautiful place one could
behold.
I wanted to stay here forever.
He smiled at me and spoke.
"You may rest now," He said softly as I dropped to my
knees.
"You may rest in this peaceful place for eternity."
My soul was filled with more content
Than I ever thought possible.
He had said, "Trust me."
He had brought me through trials.
And He had finally led me home.

(Karen's Test, *100*)

Karen had been refined in "the furnace of affliction" (Isaiah 48:10), and through the hardships, the image of God shone brightly.

We all face personalized obstacles in our life. I know that God is aware of our challenges. But if Christ were to come to earth this very moment, put his arms tightly around each of us, as I know he will someday, he would utter words similar to those he said to the Nephites shortly after his resurrection. "Therefore let your light so shine before this people, that they may see your good works and glorify your Father who is in heaven" (3 Nephi 12:16). Your own life may be the closest thing to the Savior that some people will ever know. We don't have a moment to lose sight of how important it is to have the image of God, and of Christ, *engraven* in our countenances. Christ depends on us to reflect his perfect life, so that we too can stand as a witness that he lives, that his Church is upon the earth, and that he loves us.

Lisa Olsen was born in Berkeley, California, and moved to Provo, Utah, at age eight. She served a mission in Geneva, Switzerland, and later graduated from BYU with degrees in art and French. She currently teaches art at Timpview High School, where she is also junior class advisor. She has been involved with Especially for Youth since 1983 and loves the youth programs. She and her husband, Brent, are the proud parents of Cole and Sierra.

15

ARE YOU GOING THROUGH THE MOTIONS?

Jack Marshall

In the Church, we have our own unique way of doing things. I like to refer to this lifestyle as *Cultural Mormonism.* We have learned this Latter-day Saint subculture by association and habit, by association with our fellow members and by habit through repetition. For instance, we have our own language in the Church, called "Mormonese." The favorite word in that language is *special.* When we want to use a superlative to describe an exceedingly wonderful soul, we say, "She is so special!" We never simply have a musical number in sacrament meeting; it is always a "special" musical number by Sister Mary Poppins, she's so "special." Imagine someone unfamiliar with Mormonese trying to make sense out of this announcement: "This Tuesday night, the priests, laurels, teachers, mia maids, deacons, and beehives will be baptized for the dead, after which the priesthood will lay hands upon them and confirm them!" If you don't understand Mormonese, having hands laid on you sounds kind of violent and scary, don't you think?

How about the slang term for the standard works, "a triple combination." I had a friend who was not of the faith who asked if "a triple combination" was an ice cream sundae. It made sense to me that my nonlingual friend would come to such an erroneous conclusion, considering that we fellow Saints constantly speak of going to the "stake house," not to mention the enormous servings of red punch and cookies we devour at Church dances! Long ago, as an investigator, I concluded that Joseph Smith, the Book of Mormon, and red punch and cookies were all signs of the true church! We love to eat in this church of ours, if you haven't noticed. We start our members in junk food intake training at a young age, typically in Primary. In nursery we stuff the little sweeties full of an assortment of chocolates, sugars, frosted cereals, gummy worms, and things even my ten-year-old son's dog, "Ruddy," would gag on. (And believe me, it's gotta be pretty nasty stuff to set off Ruddy's gag reflexes.) LDS could stand for Lunch, Dinner, and Supper!

There's another intriguing behavior we have in the Church, which we've learned through association and habit. The next time a tiny, sweet, sleeping baby is blessed and given a name, observe why the peaceful slumberee suddenly becomes a shrieking child from the underworld. As soon as the "brethren" get their hands cradled under the sleeping angel, as if a switch is thrown, they begin to bounce the little bundle of joy wildly up and down. As soon as the child responds with a whimper, the speed with which it is being bounced is immediately increased to warp ten, sending the little cherub into hysterical howls that catch the attention of dogs blocks away! The brethren just don't get it!

Cultural Mormonism gives rise to jokes, such as: How many ward members does it take to change a lightbulb?

Relief Society: Four—

One to change the bulb
One to bring the tablecloth
One to bring the centerpiece
One to bring the refreshments

High priests: Four—
One to change the bulb
Two to hold the wheelchair
One to hold the oxygen tank

Bishops: None—
Bishops do not change lightbulbs;
They call a ward council and assign the elders to do the
   job

Elders: Four—
One to change the bulb
Three won't show up

Home teachers: Only one—
But it will not be done until the last day of the month

Teenagers: Only one—
To hold the bulb in the socket, while the world revolves
   around them

Well, enough of these examples of our peculiar Mormon culture. The idea is simply that we learn our culture by associating with other members and by observing repetitive or habitual behavior. What I'd like to zero in on is what I call *Religious Mormonism*. Religious Mormonism is made up of the distinctive ways in which we as Latter-day Saints worship or show respect to Heavenly Father and his Son Jesus Christ. If we're not careful, we are in danger of learning how to worship in the same way we learn our culture, that is, by association and habit, rather than by sincere intent.

Learning religious behavior simply by habit is to practice institutional religion; in other words, we can be active in the Church but not active in the gospel. Here's an example or two of what I mean. Take prayers, for instance.

In the Church we have our own prayer language. Whether we live north, south, east, or west, we Mormons often use the same phrases in our prayers. "Bless this food that it will nourish and strengthen our bodies and do us the good that we need . . . and bless the hands that have prepared it." Now that prayer is fine, unless you're praying over a triple-decker banana split with chocolate and marshmallow sauce dripping off of it. I can imagine the angels in their heavenly realm above smiling at that one, saying, "Right, you eat that, and you're going to have such a sugar rush you'll be sitting up in the middle of the night screaming out scriptures!" I also get a charge out of the part about blessing the "hands." Nothing else, Heavenly Father, just their hands. Can you picture your mom in the kitchen, feverishly working over the food, when all of a sudden she shouts out, "Oh, my hands, they feel so blessed!" Don't get me wrong. I am not making fun of prayers. The scriptures teach us that what counts is that prayers be said with "real intent" (see Moroni 7:6).

What I am talking about are the "vain repetitions" referred to by the Savior in 3 Nephi 13:7. I call these vain and repetitious prayers the "Rubba dub dub, thanks for the grub" type of prayers. I don't know how many times one of my seminary students has closed class on Fridays by praying, "Please bless those who couldn't be here today, to be here tomorrow." Remember it's Friday! If that part of the prayer were answered, there would be five to ten kids standing in front of an empty, locked seminary building on Saturday, totally bewildered and mumbling to themselves, "Why am I here?"

Often you will hear this prayer phrase: "Bless us that no harm or accident will befall us." How often do you use or even hear that archaic word *befall* in your daily language? When's the last time your dad said to you, "You be home at midnight, lest any harm befall you!"? How about the phrase, "Bless the sick and afflicted"? When was the last time you answered the question, "How are you today?" by saying, "I feel sick, and also rather afflicted"? The point is this, we don't talk that way, so don't talk to Heavenly Father that way. That's institutional religion or simply going through the motions of religion. Praying in that way takes no thought. We are simply repeating what everyone else says rather than sincerely communicating with our Heavenly Father. I had a friend who taught religion classes at a prison. He said the inmates did some real belly laughing when a fellow prisoner would pray, " . . . and bless that those who can't be here today will be here tomorrow," or "We are grateful that we have this building to meet in."

Going insincerely through the motions of religion creates three detriments to spiritual growth: superficial testimony, shallow conversion, and scriptural illiteracy. Learning religious behavior by rote or habit leads to stories such as this: A young man was being interviewed by a Church leader to go on his mission. His interview was lengthy because he had violated many of the commandments. When his leader asked, "During the time you were transgressing, did you know that it was wrong?" the young man responded, "Yes." His leader then asked, "Why did you do it, if you knew that it was wrong?" He replied somewhat casually, "I always knew I could repent."

That is the kind of attitude that grows out of a superficial understanding of the gospel. So-called "planned prodigalism" is one of the great evils now widely accepted by young members of the Church. It doesn't work that way. Repentance is never easy. Sin, especially when it is committed on purpose, destroys our ability to feel the promptings of the Holy Ghost. You cannot expect to waltz in to your bishop's office, make a perfunctory confession, and go quickly to the temple or on a mission. Those who think they can do so are in for a shock.

How do we get ourselves out of the ruts of hypocritical religious behavior and become a true disciple of Christ? Here's a proven method:

John 14:15 reads: "If ye love me, keep my commandments." There's the answer. Years ago, I used to think the most effective way to motivate young people to do well or stop doing wrong was through consequence-based lessons. You've heard a million of them. Lessons on the Word of Wisdom threaten cancer if you smoke or chew. Talks on chastity frighten the listener with stories of pregnancy or fatal diseases, if the law is violated. Though the warnings are true, they have little effect in changing behavior. It is rare when someone changes their course because of fear of some consequence.

The most powerful deterrent to sin is the love we feel for the Savior and Heavenly Father. As we truly love them, obedience becomes a quest, rather than an irritation.

How then do we gain a deep love for the Father and the Son? In D&C 6:36 it tells us to "Look unto me in every thought." In D&C 19:23 it says, "Learn of me, and listen to my words; walk in the meekness of my Spirit." We are to *look* to Jesus, *listen* to him, *learn* what he did, then *walk* it. That is, walk his walk and talk his talk. That is how we "Come unto me thy Savior" (D&C 19:41). We can learn to walk as he did by looking at him, listening to his words, and learning from his ministry as it is described in the Four Gospels: Matthew, Mark, Luke, and John. Reading from these sacred writings, we can stand next to him and observe him through the eyes of his disciples. Let's do that with a couple of examples from his life.

After Jesus had been cruelly battered by the Roman guards, he was led away to be crucified. As he trudged along toward Golgotha, he struggled under the thirty- or forty-pound weight of the wooden beam to which he would be nailed. Already weakened by his three to four hours of incomprehensible suffering in Gethsemane the night before, plus the whipping, anciently referred to as the "half-death," administered by Pilate's men, Jesus finally collapsed. Mark 15:21 reads: "And they compel one Simon a Cyrenian, who passed by, coming out of the country, the father of Alexander and Rufus, to bear his cross." Cyrene was a town in Libya, a country lying on the northern coast of Africa, a great distance from Jerusalem.

Cyrene was home to a large Jewish settlement, and Simon was probably a Jew. In Jerusalem during the Passover, he suddenly came face to face with Jesus, most likely for the first time. Compelled by the soldiers, he hefted the wooden beam and walked side by side with this stranger who was on the way to his death.

Simon is not heard from again in the scriptures till the book of Romans. There, the Apostle Paul addresses members of the Church in Rome in a letter, years after Jesus' death, saying: "Salute [greet] Rufus chosen in the Lord, and his mother and mine" (Romans 16:13). Elder Neal A. Maxwell has said that the Rufus mentioned in that verse is the son of Simon the Cyrenian (see "A More Determined Discipleship," *BYU Speeches of the Year, 1978,* 156). As the Savior and Simon walked together that fateful day, Jesus must have somehow reached out and taught Simon, whose life was never the same afterward. He became a disciple. Do you think there were things other than missionary work on Jesus' mind that day as he was being led to be crucified? I love the Lord for that selfless deed. As I look, listen, and learn from Jesus, it makes me want to be a more loyal follower.

As we think about how we should live, there is another example from Jesus' life that we can consider. At one point, as he hung in agony on the cross, Jesus "cried with a loud voice, saying, Eli, Eli, lama sabachthani? that is to say, My God, my God, why hast thou forsaken me?" (Matthew 27:46). Elder Melvin J. Ballard has said of this event: "In that hour I think I can see our dear Father behind the veil looking upon these dying struggles until even he could not endure it any longer; and, like the mother who bids farewell to her dying child, has to be taken out of the room so as not to look upon the last struggles, so he bowed his head and hid in some part of his universe, his heart almost breaking for the love that he had for his son . . . " (Bryant S. Hinckley, *Sermons and Missionary Services of Melvin J. Ballard* [1949], 154).That the Father could watch those terrible last moments and not move to rescue his son, helps us to better appreciate these words: "For God so loved the world, that he gave his only begotten Son" (John 3:16).

I remember an experience I had when I was ten years old. I was playing in my front yard with some friends when our game was interrupted by some passing fire trucks. Lights flashing and sirens blaring, they roared past my house. In the lead truck was my dad, who was the fire marshal in our community. We of course hustled to our bicycles, and off we sped in hot pursuit of the fire engines. As we peddled furiously, we could see black billowing smoke ahead of us, rising over the tree line of the neighborhood. Something big had erupted into a blazing inferno. As we rounded the corner onto another street, we saw it! A house was totally engulfed in flames!

The blaze was lapping up from under the eves of the roof and surging from every window, which had all been blown out by heat so intense that we could feel it, even though we were a long distance away. A large crowd gathered, and I proudly watched as my dad directed his men in fighting back the flames. Suddenly, there was a sound of squealing tires, and a car rounded the corner of the street. The car straightened then roared toward the crowd, screeching to a halt just short of us. The doors of the automobile flew open, and a woman jumped out, clinging to the car door and hysterically calling out names. A man sprinted from the driver's side of the car, running toward the burning house, screaming the same names. My father later told me these were the parents of two children who had been left with a sitter that night as the couple went on a date. The sitter was the one who saw the fire starting, called 911, and rushed the children out. Their children were safe, but the parents weren't aware. I observed the love that an imperfect, mortal parent can have for his child as I watched the father race to save his children. He was about to charge into an inferno without regard for his safety, but my father and two other firemen tackled the frantic man and held him down on the ground. He was calmed and burst into tears when told that his children were safe. The mother's response was the same when she was told the comforting news.

I've read newspaper accounts of parents or children who couldn't swim a stroke, throwing themselves into raging rivers to save a loved one. I don't think it would be too dramatic or an overstatement to say that some of you reading this book would do the same for someone you deeply loved. That is the type of devotion an imperfect human can feel and experience. Then we reflect upon a perfect Father in Heaven who, watching his son suffer beyond comprehension and hearing him plead for aid, restrained himself from coming down and rescuing him. That is the infinite love of a God. Had he delivered his son in Gethsemane when he pled, "Father, all things are possible unto thee; take away this cup from me" (Mark 14:36), there would have been no payment for our sins. After our first foolish, rebellious mistake we would have been instantly doomed—subjected forever to Satan's punishments. Had Heavenly Father freed Jesus from the cruel nails driven through him, as he begged, "My God, my God, why hast thou forsaken me?" (Matthew 27:46), or had Jesus used his power and brought himself down from the cross, there would have been no resurrection. From the moment death stole away a brother, sister, mom, dad, or a grandparent, we would never have the opportunity to see or talk to or hold them again. I love Heavenly Father and Jesus for that sacrifice.

We'll overcome our weaknesses and tendencies to go through the motions, only by first coming to love the Father and the Son. They will make more out of us than we'll ever make of ourselves. Referring to the Savior's promise that we might have "life" (see John 5:40), Sister Patricia Holland asked, "What does he mean when he softly scolds, 'Ye will not come to me, that ye might have life'? I don't think he was just talking about life eternal (though that too). I think he was speaking about here and now. I think he was speaking about a constant feeling of well-being and of thanksgiving for our very existence, of being alive spiritually. I think he was saying that we search everywhere else for it first. We search for it in the praise of men, in worldly treasures or worldly pleasures, in clothing, in dances, in enormous amounts of pizza, while all the time he is crying, 'Come unto me, and ye will have life'" (President's Assembly, Marriott Center, BYU, September 7, 1982).

That we might have such life, through Jesus Christ, is my prayer for each of us.

 *Jack Marshall lives in Bountiful, Utah, and teaches institute at the University of Utah. He holds a bachelor's degree from Weber State College and a master's degree from BYU. Brother Marshall has worked for the Church Educational System for twenty-four years and has lectured widely for the BYU Department of Continuing Education. He has had articles published in the* New Era *and the* Ensign. *Jack is married to Liz Johnson, and they are the parents of five children.*

16

PATRIARCHAL BLESSINGS

Cliff Rhoades

Several years ago, during the Christmas season, I went into the mountains of Utah with a good friend to find and cut a Christmas tree. As is the nature of all true seekers of the "perfect tree," my friend and I wandered from one prospective tree to another, searching for the "right one." Since it took some time to drive to where the best trees grew, the sun was almost setting when Jack and I started our search. After going from one tree to the next, before finding the right one, we had wandered quite a way from the road, and it had now become quite dark. We weren't prepared for a night hike and neither of us had a flashlight. But with the "perfect tree" acquired, Jack and I started back to where we thought we had left the truck. We walked for quite some time but didn't come to where we thought the road should be. I remember Jack saying that either someone had moved the road or we were lost. About that time, a set of car lights came on for a couple of minutes and then went off. The lights were located at about a ninety-degree angle to our right. Since we were getting cold and the direction we were heading didn't look too promising, we headed for the lights. Every so often, the lights would come on and then go off, and we would make an adjustment in the direction we were going. By periodically adjusting our direction, we arrived at the place where we had parked the truck. Fortunately for us, one of Jack's children had wanted to come get the tree with us, and since we were not going to be very long, opted to stay warm in the truck while we conducted our search. When Jack and I didn't come back with the tree before dark, Jack Jr. figured we were lost and would periodically turn the truck lights on and off in the hope that it would do just what it did—guide us back to safety.

I share this experience with you to make a point about what a patriarchal blessing can do for each one of us. Just as the light that came periodically from my truck headlights guided Jack and me to safety, one's patriarchal blessing can guide him or her through this life back to our heavenly home.

Patriarchal blessings have been part of the gospel since Adam, and one can find references to such blessings in each of the standard works. For example, in Ephesians 4:11 there is a reference to *evangelists*. In the Bible Dictionary we are told that an evangelist is a patriarch (see D&C 107:39–53). An analysis of the word *patriarch* itself provides an understanding of the kind of guidance our Heavenly Father desires to give us. *Patri* means *father,* and *Arch* means *chief.* You can see that Heavenly Father has given us another "father" on this earth. Therefore, in the Church of Jesus Christ, we have two fathers, our natural father, to whom we are born, and an ordained father. Both can give us blessings, but in most cases, only the ordained father can pronounce on us the blessings that are a part of the Abrahamic covenant. The patriarch can also pronounce the lineage of the recipient, that is, which of the families of Israel an individual is descended from or into which that person is adopted. To better understand the concept of lineage, look at the diagram below:

Abraham
|
Isaac
|
Jacob (Israel)
|
Reuben, Simeon, Levi, Judah, Issachar, Zebulun, Dan, Gad, Asher, Naphtali, Joseph, Benjamin
|
Manasseh, Ephraim

When Jacob's name was changed to Israel by the Lord, each of his twelve sons then became the head of one of the twelve tribes of Israel (see Genesis 32:28). Later on, after Joseph and Jacob were reunited in Egypt, Joseph asked Jacob to bless his two sons, Ephraim and Manasseh. This is the famous cross-hands blessing recounted in Genesis 48:5–22. To summarize what happened: Joseph brought his two sons to Jacob for a patriarchal blessing and had them both kneel down in front of Jacob at the same time. Manasseh was the eldest and was positioned so that Jacob's *right* hand would naturally rest on Manasseh's head. Being younger, Ephraim was caused to kneel in a position to be under Jacob's *left* hand. The arrangement of the two sons is significant. The blessing given under the right hand would be the birthright blessing, and as the oldest of the two, it would have normally fallen on Manasseh.

Jacob was old at the time and was losing his eyesight, and when the old man crossed his hands, putting his right hand on Ephraim, Joseph protested. He attempted to reverse his father's hands, to put them in what would have been the proper order, but Jacob indicated he knew what he was doing, and pronounced the birthright blessing on Ephraim. In the blessing that followed, Jacob literally adopted the two sons of Joseph into the tribes of Israel and placed them in leadership positions at the head of two of the twelve tribes—Ephraim replacing Reuben and Manasseh replacing Simeon. In the blessing, Jacob gave his grandsons leadership responsibilities, with Ephraim taking the primary role and Manasseh helping. Their responsibility is to preside over and direct the work of God's covenant people.

Those who are descended from these two, or who are adopted into that lineage, are charged with the responsibility to find, teach, and baptize members of the house of Israel. Somewhere in most patriarchal blessings given in our day, there is usually some mention of leadership responsibility. The patriarch also frequently bestows the "blessings of Abraham, Isaac, and Jacob" on the recipient (see D&C 84:33–40).

Patriarchal blessings are sometimes difficult to interpret. Blessings pronounced on the recipient may not be realized immediately or perhaps not even in this lifetime. One should not be upset if something is promised in a blessing that appears to have no way of happening in this mortal life. Remember, patriarchal blessings are like brief flashes of light that help guide us until we return unto the Father.

President Joseph Fielding Smith stated the following on this concept: "My uncle, John Smith, who gave as many blessings I suppose as anybody, said one day to me in the presence of others, 'When I give a patriarchal blessing, the dividing line between time and eternity disappears.' . . . There may be things in these blessings that pertain to our future existence. There might be promises made to us that are not fulfilled here that will be fulfilled. For instance, suppose a patriarch in giving a blessing to a young woman promises that she will be married and that she will have posterity, and she dies without posterity. Married for time and all eternity in the temple of our Lord, she receives there the blessings of eternal lives, which is a continuation of the seeds forever. Perhaps the patriarch, in giving her a blessing of posterity, sees beyond the veil; so I don't think we should be too hasty in condemning a patriarch when he promises posterity, and then in this life that blessing is not fulfilled. We may ourselves be at fault in judging in matters of that kind" (The Church of Jesus Christ of Latter-day Saints, *Teachings of the Latter-day Prophets* [1986], 460).

Elder John A. Widtsoe further states: "There must be no quibbling about the time or place when the promises should be fulfilled or about the man who gave it. As the blessing was given through the inspiration of the Lord, so its meaning will be made clear by the same power; and its fulfillment will be in His hands. Above all, it must be remembered that every blessing is conditioned upon our faithfulness" (Rulon T. Burton, *We Believe* [1994], 622). If your blessing doesn't contain something that you think should be in there, it doesn't mean that it will or will not happen. For example, if your blessing doesn't contain anything about going on a mission, it doesn't mean that you shouldn't go or won't be called. It has been already revealed to you from a prophet of God what you should do.

Perhaps to understand President Smith's and Elder Widtsoe's statements, it would be helpful to understand the difference between predestination and foreordination. Predestination is a false doctrine, which says that certain people are predestined to behave in certain ways or to accomplish certain things in life. This doctrine holds that those who are predestined are powerless to change the course of things. God's will compels events to transpire and things to take place. The Church of Jesus Christ of Latter-day Saints DOES NOT believe in predestination. To be predestined would mean that everything in your life is *destined* to happen and that you have no choice or option to do anything about it. Predestination ignores the marvelous gift of agency, which is a basic principle in the gospel of Jesus Christ and in the Plan of Salvation. The promises made to you in your patriarchal blessing should not be viewed as inevitable. We claim such blessings based on righteous behavior and our willingness to keep the commandments. The patriarch is really declaring our *potential.* It is up to us to live in such a way to be worthy of all God has in store for us.

Foreordination is a true doctrine, which was taught by Joseph Smith: "Every man who has a calling to minister to the inhabitants of the world was ordained to that very purpose in the Grand Council of heaven before this world was" (*Teachings of the Prophet Joseph Smith* [1954], 365). Patriarchs are often blessed with inspiration to identify these important callings in the blessings they pronounce on members of the Church.

To gain a better understanding of your eternal you, try this little exercise with your patriarchal blessing. Take a piece of paper and divide it into three columns. In the first column put the heading "WHO AM I?" Then, as you read through your blessing, put statements about you, your potential, your foreordained mission, the relationship you had with the Father, professions or occupations that may be suggested or hinted at, and anything that states or gives an impression of who you were in the premortal life or what positions you might have held there. In the next column put "PROMISES AND BLESSINGS." In this column, list any promise or blessing that the Father reveals to you and the conditions upon which these promises and blessings are dependent. In the last column put "WARNINGS AND COUNSEL." Here you can list any counsel, warnings, reminders, suggestions, or cautions that Heavenly Father gives to you.

After you've done this, turn the paper over. On that side, make two columns. At the top of one column, put "TALENTS AND SKILLS I NOW HAVE." Since most young people shortchange themselves and often feel as though they have no talents or skills whatsoever, ask some friends, teachers, or family members to help you fill in this column. Write down all the attributes these people say. Don't judge yourself. If they say you have a warm smile, a positive outlook, or are a faithful friend, write it down. Chances are, these talents, skills, and abilities are those you brought with you from the premortal world. They are being fine-tuned here in mortality. This should give you some insight into the type of person you are.

In the other column, put "TALENTS AND SKILLS I WISH I HAD." This column has to be filled in by you alone, following a time of serious reflection. This is where you prayerfully look into your heart to define the kind of person you would like to be. I believe that every human being has at least one "dream of the heart"—something Heavenly Father will help you accomplish if you desire it enough and will work to make it a reality. It may take years to develop or even a lifetime, but you will have at least identified it.

Here are some other things to consider, having to do

with patriarchal blessings. One of the most common questions asked is, at what age should I obtain my patriarchal blessing? Elder Eldred G. Smith, who served for many years as Patriarch to the Church, answers that question: "I think the best age is between fifteen and twenty-five. However, every baptized member of the Church is entitled to receive a patriarchal blessing. He should be old enough to understand the meaning and purpose and value of a patriarchal blessing to the extent that he has a personal desire to receive such a blessing, and not because a group is getting blessings, or because friends or neighbors are getting blessings, or because an adult or parent has the desire that the child should receive a blessing" (in Conference Report, April 1960, 66). There needs to be a certain level of maturity and sufficient personal spiritual preparation for one to obtain this blessing. One should never seek a patriarchal blessing out of mere curiosity or to fulfill some requirement. The best time to obtain a patriarchal blessing is when the Spirit says to and when you have developed an honest desire to know the Lord's will concerning you.

Once you acquire this personal desire, the first step is to contact your bishop and ask to have a patriarchal blessing interview. This would be a good time to "clean the slate" or become as worthy as you can so that the Spirit of the Lord will not be restrained in your behalf. One patriarch in Idaho shared an experience about a young man who had a foul mouth. The boy had been in to see his bishop and had been given the recommend to receive his blessing, but when the patriarch put his hands on this young man's head, the patriarch's mind went blank. There was no inspiration. He removed his hands, then replaced them in an effort to try again. Once more, he had no blessing to give. Finally, he told the youth that the Lord was silent and that there must be something that needed to be resolved within the life of the youth before the blessing could be given. Several months later, after the youth had taken steps to put his life in order, he came back to the patriarch and received a beautiful blessing. Be as worthy as you can and once you obtain the recommend from your bishop, contact the patriarch in your stake to secure a time for the blessing.

Typically, the time will be within a two-week period following your interview with your bishop. You might use that two-week period to prepare yourself through prayer, scripture reading, and appropriate fasting. Go to your appointment with a prayer in your heart—for both the patriarch and for you—that you might receive the blessing the Lord has in store for you. If you desire, you may have your parents accompany you. In keeping with the sacredness of the occasion, it would be well to wear your Sunday clothes, even if the blessing is given on some other day of the week.

Because of the sacred nature of these blessings, the patriarch will record the blessing to ensure accuracy. You will be given a written copy of your blessing and a duplicate copy will be sent to Church headquarters where it will be kept on file. In the event you lose your copy, you can obtain a duplicate by making a request.

Young people are often tempted to share the content of their blessing with friends. What has been promised you is sacred and highly personal. It is meant for you and not for others to read. You should keep it in a safe place and refer to it often, but showing it to others serves no purpose. You may wish to share it with your parents or discuss it with your bishop and (eventually) your spouse. Beyond that, allow the Spirit to direct you to let you know with whom the blessing should be shared. Avoid comparing yours with others in any situation where the Spirit of the Lord isn't present. Some worry that their blessing is too short or not specific enough. You are an individual, and you are unique. The Lord will reveal to you what *you* need to know about your journey through life. Some people need a bit more insight than others. Seek to understand your blessing and trust that the Lord has revealed all that you need to know. If you have a hard time understanding the meaning to your blessing, the best place to go is to the author of the blessing himself, your Heavenly Father.

In order to maximize its effect and power in your life, I challenge you to memorize your blessing and to review it often. As you do so, the windows of your understanding will be opened, and you will come to know the deeper meanings of your patriarchal blessing.

Cliff Rhoades has been a seminary instructor for twelve years and has worked with the BYU Department of Religion for three. He was converted to the Church at age twenty-two and later served a mission in Ventura, California. Cliff and his wife were married in the Idaho Falls Temple and have four daughters. He has been a survival teacher, and he loves all outdoor activities. A former bishop, he serves currently in his stake Young Men presidency.

17

ARE WE NOT ALL BEGGARS–WHAT SIGN DO YOU SEE?

Vance Yoshikawa

Christmas of 1991 will always be special to me. That was the Christmas the Spirit taught me how to focus more closely on the Savior during the holiday when we celebrate his birth. I was teaching seminary at a junior high school in the Salt Lake Valley. One Monday night my wife and I took our nineteen-month-old daughter to Temple Square to see the Christmas lights. As we were driving through town, I noticed a number of individuals holding up cardboard signs asking for help. There was nothing unusual about that, but at that season of the year, the needs of these people seemed especially great. Scrawled on the signs were such appeals as: "Will Work for Food"; "Please Help"; "Homeless."

As we continued our trek toward the lights, I noticed a number of other signs. Various fast-food operations were advertising: "Now hiring $5.00/hour"; "Jobs available $6.00/hour"; "Looking for employment? Inquire within." I thought to myself, *Why don't you guys put your cardboard signs down and talk to those people who might hire you?* I have to admit that I wasn't feeling any too charitable. In my mind, these beggars were just too lazy to walk across the street and find a way to help themselves.

Arriving at Temple Square, we bundled up and prepared to go in and enjoy the lights and displays. As we entered the gates, I couldn't help noticing others who were seeking help. A couple of them had laid their open guitar cases on the ground, soliciting coins in return for the music they were playing. We passed by them and entered the brightly lit square, where the lights, Christmas music, and festive atmosphere provided a way for me to teach my daughter a lesson about the Savior and the miracle of his birth. We went home feeling as though we had given Ashley a good experience.

The next day, while preparing my lesson for seminary, I was reading in Mosiah, chapter four, where it says in verse 16, "And also, ye yourselves will succor those that stand in need of your succor." It struck me that *succor* was a strange word, but the footnote referred me to some related words in the Topical Guide: *charity, service,* and *welfare.* So, in other words, we are to provide charity for those who need charity; service for those who need service; and welfare for those who need welfare.

The verse continues: "Ye will administer of your substance unto him that standeth in need; and ye will not suffer that the beggar putteth up his petition to you in vain, and turn him out to perish." Immediately, I thought about my experience of the preceding night, and I was conscience struck. My guilt overwhelmed me to the point where I did not think I could continue in my reading, but I knew I needed to.

Verse 17 goes on, "Perhaps thou shalt say: The man has brought upon himself his misery; therefore I will stay my hand, and will not give unto him of my food, nor impart unto him of my substance that he may not suffer, for his punishments are just." Immediately, my uncharitable thoughts of the previous night returned. Without knowing their circumstances, I had judged those people and concluded that if they were too lazy to work, they deserved to be out in the cold.

I love my wife and child. I felt that I was a temple worthy priesthood holder. I was trying to do all that I could to live the gospel. I was hoping that I would live with my family forever. But, as I read verse 18, I knew I had some repenting to do. "But I say unto you, O man, whosoever doeth this the same hath great cause to repent; and except he repenteth of that which he hath done he perisheth forever, and hath no interest in the kingdom of God." The words "perisheth forever," and "hath no interest in the kingdom of God," sunk deep into my soul. I felt low enough to crawl under the door.

My wife is the most understanding human being I know, but when I telephoned her from my office, she was confused.

"Zoeanne, we need to go to Temple Square tonight."

"We went last night," she replied.

"I know, but we need to go and find a homeless person." She didn't respond for a moment, but she agreed to go after I told her I would explain in more detail after I got home.

That night, we dropped Ashley off at the baby-sitter's and returned to Temple Square. On the way, we stopped by an ATM and withdrew a little cash. As we drove through the streets, the people with cardboard signs seemed to be scarcer. In fact, we circled Temple Square several times without finding anyone who looked to be "homeless." We searched for a long time. Finally, we noticed two disheveled men, walking east up the north side of the Square, who seemed to fit the description. I stopped the car, right in the middle of the street, and jumped out to talk to them. Zoeanne got out of the car and into the driver's seat to park the car and happened to find a parking space a little further on.

She was getting out of the car by the time I got to where she parked, and we ran together to catch the men. You know how your heart beats when the Spirit urges you to get up and bear your testimony? That's how I felt as we rounded the corner onto Main Street on the east side of Temple Square. My heart was beating so hard, it made me kind of breathless. Then, we saw something disturbing. One of the men we had been trying to catch was down on his knees, being handcuffed by a policeman. The officer had the man's hands pulled behind his back and his face pushed against the cold cement. The man's friend was standing nearby, leaning against the wall, with a very embarrassed look on his face. People passing by glanced at the scene and hurried on. Zoeanne asked me what we should do, and I had no answer.

As we got closer to where the man was kneeling, I noticed him wincing in discomfort. I could see he was missing his front teeth and his face was badly bruised.

The scene seemed to be unfolding in slow motion. Suddenly, I made eye contact with the injured man, and an overwhelming feeling came over me that this man was a child of God. He was a child of God, and he was indeed my brother.

I knew then what King Benjamin meant in verse 19 when he stated, "For behold, are we not all beggars? Do we not all depend upon the same Being, even God, for all the substance which we have. . . . "

We walked past the scene to the corner and waited. As we stood there, I couldn't help but remember the things I had read in the Book of Mormon. After a few minutes, the man was released and he began walking toward us, holding a Styrofoam cup in his hand. When he got to where we were, I reached out and dropped some money in his cup. He wasn't panhandling. As a matter of fact, he looked somewhat ashamed, probably because of the indignity of what he had just experienced. He looked at me and, with a tear in his eye, said, "Merry Christmas, God bless you." I have never seen that man since.

Before I continue, I must state that it is not wise (nor is it expected) to give all your money away to every person asking for a handout. There are other ways to help. Nor do

I feel that you should put yourself in a dangerous situation that might jeopardize your safety. What I feel King Benjamin is telling us to do is something much deeper.

I knew I had learned a lesson. Being a teacher, I wanted to share this lesson with my students in an effective way. My bishop has a lot of costumes, and I occasionally borrow some for one reason or another. I went to his house and told him I needed to borrow some clothes in order to dress like a homeless person. Judging by the look on his face, I probably could have asked him in a better way.

The next morning was brisk. Dressed in my homeless garb, I lay down outside the chain-link fence that surrounds our seminary building. I was about thirty feet from the main door and out of the way of the students who would be entering the building. However, I was in plain sight of anyone going to seminary. Between the other teacher and myself, there would be around 300 ninth-grade students who would be coming to seminary within seven periods. There were one or two classes being taught in the seminary each period, and between each class period, I did my little act. My attire consisted of a pair of old boots, winter overalls, a denim jacket with the collar turned up on the sides and in the back, and a stocking cap pulled down over my face. I wrapped myself in a blanket and lay down with my back up against the fence on the cold hard ground. Not one of the students recognized me.

As soon as students began to approach, I would move around as though I were trying to get comfortable. I was lying only about five feet from the sidewalk, so they could easily see me. Since I was moving around, it was clear also that I wasn't dead. To my surprise, during the entire day, only one student out of 300 asked me if I was okay. I'm sorry to report that I was subjected to some things that ought to embarrass Latter-day Saints. I had snowballs thrown at me. Some students kicked at me through the fence. A few students even spit on me. Unfortunately, I was called every four-letter word in the book. Most students simply ignored me.

It was heartwarming that a few students responded charitably. One young woman offered me a peanut butter sandwich. Being a wonderful person, she said, "Here, sir, you can have the rest of my lunch." One boy tossed part of a bag of *Skittles* to me, with a remark that I needed them more than he did. He was alone, and I sensed his sincerity. These unselfish acts were committed by students in my fifth period, and both gestures brought a tear to my eye.

While I was outside experiencing the life of a homeless person, my students proceeded with the devotional. The purpose was to try and "invite the Spirit" into the classroom. When the devotional was over, the door to the classroom opened and the homeless man entered the classroom. He removed his stocking cap, and the students recognized the face of their teacher. A few students sunk down in their seats with the discovery. The room was dead silent as students dealt with various thoughts racing through their minds. It was an experience that neither my students, nor I, will forget. Some students ashamedly asked me if I had recognized their voices or knew who had kicked me. I told them I had recognized some of their voices, but that wasn't the important thing. What they needed to know was that Heavenly Father knew who had been kind and who hadn't. The stage was now set to learn from King Benjamin.

We talked about people in the school who, for whatever reason, were judged by others to be "different." I asked them to think about those they were quick to label "geeks" or "nerds"—people in their wards, neighborhoods, and other places whom the scriptures might identify as "beggars." We discovered together that King Benjamin was talking about "beggars" in a spiritual sense as well as a literal sense. Some of the signs that spiritual beggars might display include, "Help, I Need a Friend"; "Will Work for Love"; "Live in a House, but I'm Still Homeless"; "Please Talk to Me."

It is probably not wise to give all our money away or to approach every stranger we encounter. But, I do feel that as a covenant people it is essential to be looking out for our brothers and sisters. We need to take care of those in and out of the Church. We need to take care of both active and less active members. It is up to us to use our spiritual eyes and pay attention to the *spiritual cardboard signs* of others.

Whenever Latter-day Saints are present, there should never be anyone feeling self-conscious about themselves. For example, a girl sits sadly in the corner of a dance as she misses out on another song. A boy retreats into the hallway, too scared to talk to anyone for fear of being ridiculed. A student in the lunchroom sits alone. People stay home alone because they feel no one wants to include them. These are people holding spiritual cardboard signs. There are many more examples that would fit your own situation. All of us hold our own signs up at different times in our lives. We only need to ask our Father in Heaven to help us see more clearly the signs that are being held.

In verse 21 King Benjamin states, "And now, if God, who has created you, on whom you are dependent for your lives and for all that ye have and are, doth grant unto you whatsoever ye ask that is right, in faith, believing that ye shall receive, O then, how ye ought to impart of the substance that ye have one to another."

The ability to help others varies with circumstances. Some of us have limited resources. We simply *can't* give to everyone who asks. The Lord knows that. Consider what King Benjamin says in the last part of verse 24: "I mean all you who deny the beggar, because ye have not; I would that ye say in your hearts that: I give not because I have not, but if I had I would give." I'm sure that many of the students who walked by me and said or did nothing simply didn't know what to do or had nothing to give. Some people are so full of love, they hurt for others in their hearts when they see people in pain. We should have enough charity to desire to help all. But know that we will not be accountable for not helping when we have not.

Those who want to do everything they possibly can for

everyone they come across, or feel guilty for not being able to act, consider verse 27: "And see that all these things are done in wisdom and order; for it is not requisite that a man should run faster than he has strength." We should be careful not to spread ourselves too thin by trying to do everything for everyone. As members of the Church, we can do much to help the poor by contributing a generous fast offering, an inspired program that is part of the "wisdom and order" of the Lord.

King Benjamin's words are as applicable today as they were when they were given. I would hope that we will continually strive to help and love another. For "are we not all beggars?" In our struggle to make it back to our Father in Heaven, some of us may get lost and wander off the path that will lead us there. Along the way, we may encounter friends who hold up their spiritual cardboard signs in an attempt to get a little help. Let us not pass by them, but rather remove their need by our actions and by our thoughtfulness. Through abiding by his words, may we all come to know more fully the significance of the birth of the Savior. May we also have that Christmas feeling in our hearts every day of the year and not just one day in December. I testify that our Father lives, and we are all his children who depend on him for all that we have and are.

Vance Yoshikawa was born in Florida, but has lived in Utah since he was four years old. He joined the Church at age seventeen (his family are still not members). After graduating from Layton High School, he served a mission in Tokyo, Japan. Later he graduated from Weber State with a degree in family relations. Vance was sealed to Zoeanne Teeples in August 1988 and has four wonderful children. He has served in many Church callings and is currently on the high council of the Kearns Utah West Stake. He has taught seminary for three years.

18

SCRIPTURE POWER

Gary R. Nelson

Seventeen-year-old Lisa and her family left their home to attend a high school choir performance in which she was singing. Unknown to them, disaster struck while they were at the concert. Their old pioneer home on South Main Street caught fire in the second story. The cause was attributed to old, faulty wiring.

Passing by the home, an observant neighbor saw the black smoke billowing out of the upstairs windows and called the volunteer fire department. He quickly grabbed a garden hose in the front of the house and did what he could to quench the lapping flames by squirting a small spray of water on them. A fire engine soon arrived and extinguished the fire. The neighbors desired to notify the family but were unaware of their whereabouts.

Can you imagine the family's surprise when, after the concert, they found the fire engine leaving their yard and the entire second floor of their cherished home burned? The home had been filled with thick black smoke, and with the fire having destroyed the house's wiring, the family was without electrical power. They would have to wait until morning to see how much they had lost.

Lisa was especially concerned about the extent of the damage. When dawn arrived, she rushed up the narrow steps to her bedroom and was there devastated by what she saw. Everything in her room, including her bed, a chest of drawers, and wardrobe, was destroyed or melted. What was left of the roof above her room was charred, revealing the outside sky. All of her many clothes had either been burned or scorched beyond the point of salvage.

She looked for her school yearbooks. She had left them stacked on the carpeted floor next to her bed. They were sandwiched between her white leather book of remembrance on the bottom and her scriptures on the top. What she found was amazing! Her school yearbook covers were completely burned off and the pages of each book scorched beyond recognition. Her scriptures and book of remembrance, however, were miraculously *untouched* and as intact as she had left them! "Something had shielded them," Lisa said. "The reality of this marvelous happening did not hit me until later when I picked up my scriptures to complete a seminary assignment. They did not even smell smoky. They look perfectly new to this day!" she reported.

The sacredness of the scriptures and that which is most holy to the Lord was powerfully manifested to Lisa that night. She gained a forceful testimony of how the Lord feels about his words and the concern he has that they be protected.

THE SCRIPTURES ARE SACRED

Through the ages the Lord has communicated with his prophets. Each prophet has written the words of God as he was commanded. Many times the task of writing was difficult, laborious, and time-consuming. Despite the challenges, records were kept and preserved at great sacrifice and risk. Alma's counsel to his eldest son, Helaman, bears solemn testimony of the sacredness of the plates. "And now remember, my son, that God has entrusted you with these things, which are sacred, which he has kept sacred, and also which he will keep and preserve for a wise purpose in him, that he may show forth his *power* unto future generations" (Alma 37:14; emphasis added).

As prophet-translator, Joseph Smith not only devoted much time to translating the record, but he spent considerable time hiding the plates to keep them safe from "evil and conspiring men." The plates were hidden in places such as a hollow log, under a hearthstone, under a wooden floor in a cooper's shop, in a barn, in a hayloft, and in a barrel of beans. The adversary seemed determined to thwart the coming forth of the Book of Mormon, and the possible loss of the plates was a great and constant worry to the Prophet.

An example of the effort required to preserve sacred writings can be seen in what happened in 1833. By then, there were two main centers of gathering: Kirtland, Ohio, and Jackson County, Missouri. By July of that year, religious prejudice and misunderstanding were causing angry feelings between the original settlers in Jackson County and the Mormons who were arriving in ever-increasing numbers. Anti-Mormon sentiment led to a town meeting in the courthouse where it was decided that the Mormons would have to leave their new homes or be killed. Leaders of the opposition turned down the Latter-day Saints' offer to evacuate within three months. They also refused the Mormons' plea that they be given ten days to get out. The angry settlers demanded instead that the Saints leave immediately. They would be given only fifteen minutes!

The mob then began burning and ransacking homes, barns, and other possessions of the Saints. They entered the home of William W. Phelps, a prominent Church leader and printer. He was at that time engaged in printing the *Book of Commandments* from the Prophet Joseph Smith's original manuscripts, which were in Phelps's printing office located in the upstairs of his home. (You may recall this scene in the movie, *Legacy,* produced by the Church.) While Sister Phelps was tending a sick child, members of the mob rampaged through her home and roughly ordered her out. Seeking to thwart the publication of the *Book of Commandments,* they threw the printing press, type, and manuscript out of the upstairs window onto the street below.

Two courageous young women, fifteen-year-old Mary Elizabeth Rollins and her thirteen-year-old sister, Caroline, were watching the mayhem and ruckus and were prompted to try to save the scattered manuscript pages. When members of the mob had their backs turned, Mary and Caroline ran and snatched up armloads of the large printed sheets. Sheltering the precious pages with their bodies, the two ran into a nearby cornfield and lay down on the ground between the rows of six-foot-tall stalks. Later, they navigated their way out of the field by following the tops of the trees, and as they emerged next to an old stable, they discovered Sister Phelps, her sick baby, and her older children in hiding. Mary and Caroline gave the documents they had saved to Sister Phelps (see Maureen Ursenbach Beecher, "Discover Your Heritage: 'They Will Kill Us!'" *New Era,* September 1974, 36–37).

Can you appreciate the courage of these two young women in the preservation of these precious words of the Lord? The manuscripts they saved were published as the *Book of Commandments* in 1833, which comprised the first sixty-five sections of our present Doctrine and Covenants. Can you imagine the loss if we did not have these sections for doctrine, learning, and edification in our lives? I am personally grateful to the many who have given much to preserve the words of the Lord. The importance of this great record is declared by President Ezra Taft Benson, who said: "The Book of Mormon brings men to Christ. The Doctrine and Covenants brings men to Christ's kingdom, even The Church of Jesus Christ of Latter-day Saints . . . The Book of Mormon is the 'keystone' of our religion, and the Doctrine and Covenants is the capstone, with continuing latter-day revelation. The Lord has placed his stamp of approval on both the keystone and the capstone" (*Ensign,* May 1987, 83).

We should treat our scriptures with care and respect.

I am reminded of a young man who entered my seminary class the first day of school his senior year. He picked up his Bible from a stack of scriptures piled in the back, left there from the last day of school the previous May. I had also taught him as a junior, and he was an outstanding athlete, especially in football. But at that point in his life, he had little respect for adults and others. To say he had an "attitude problem" was a mild understatement. He said, "Bro, what is it we are studying this year in seminary?" I responded, "We studied the Old Testament last year and we are studying the New Testament this year." Hearing that, he took his black vinyl Bible and proceeded to rip the entire Old Testament out of his scriptures and hurl the pages into the trash can, announcing brashly, "I guess I don't need this part of the Bible then. This will be lots easier scripture chasing now with just the New Testament." I could have konked him. I could have offered him up as the first senior sacrifice of the year—a burnt offering—right then and there! This young man had not yet allowed the scriptures to become a part of him. Without realizing their worth to him, he irreverently disregarded and discarded them. To his credit, he finally outgrew his rebellion and learned to love and teach the sacred words of the scriptures while serving a successful mission.

Please treat your scriptures with respect. They remind us of who we are . . . where we are going . . . and how to get there! Mark them, footnote them, and use them as treasured resources. Their very existence is an evidence of the sacrifice made by many of the prophets through the ages, many of whom have sealed their testimonies with their blood (see D&C 135:3). Please remember they have come forth in these last days at a price . . . *the scriptures are sacred.*

WE ARE COMMANDED TO READ THE SCRIPTURES

It is not just enough to have a copy of the standard works: the Bible, Book of Mormon, Doctrine and Covenants, and Pearl of Great Price; we should read and study them.

The prophet Alma reminds us: "Ye ought to search the scriptures" (Alma 33:2); and President Ezra Taft Benson has said, "Immerse yourselves in the scriptures. Search them diligently. Feast upon the words of Christ. Learn the doctrine. Master the principles that are found therein. . . . Few other efforts . . . will bring greater dividends. . . . Few other ways [will result in] greater inspiration" (*Ensign,* November 1986, 47).

We encourage daily scripture study in seminary. The desired outcome is to finish reading the religious book of study for the year. Different programs for consecutive or cumulative reading are emphasized. Some recommend a ten-minute program while others encourage reading a chapter or section a day. Regardless of the program, the ultimate goal is the same: to read the scriptures every day.

Several years ago I instructed a young man at Roy High School by the name of Doug Shaw. He was a senior in the class of 1982 and was my second-period seminary class president. Doug had the debilitating disease of muscular dystrophy. He was the Utah State Muscular Dystrophy Poster Boy in 1971. His illness made it necessary for him to use an electric wheelchair; but his disease did not stop him from making the most of his life. He went on dates, blessed and passed the sacrament, and loved to play practical jokes on people. He attended all of Roy High's athletic events. Although he should have attended neighboring Weber High School, he was bussed to Roy because it offered special handicapped instruction and facilities. He was always up in the balcony in the gym or at the top of the stadium, seated in his wheelchair, waving white and gold pom-poms and cheering on his "Royals." His wheelchair was plastered with Roy High bumper stickers.

The players appreciated Doug's support and his attendance at the games and often recognized his presence by waving to him. Doug was an example and inspiration to all who knew him, both at Roy High and in his hometown of Liberty. He was voted "Most School Spirit" for the school year 1981–82. One day Doug did not show up for class. Doug never missed school, so I was surprised. It was unusual not to hear the buzz of his electric wheelchair in the seminary hallway. I called the school office and was informed Doug was at the McKay Dee Hospital in serious condition. The disease had advanced to its final stages.

Doug passed away on Thursday, January 29, 1982. He was eighteen years of age. He had a GPA of 4.0 his senior year, was on the honor roll, and was listed in *Who's Who among American High School Students.* He was also an assistant in his priests quorum presidency, the editor of his ward bulletin, and active in Boy Scouts. But even more important than all of these achievements was his testimony of the Lord, Jesus Christ. Just ten days before his passing, Doug bore a powerful witness of His divinity in our seminary class. Doug knew the Savior and had read His words. Before his death, he had read the entire New Testament and was in Romans 16, on the way to his second time through. Doug's death traumatized our school and community. It was a sorrowful time for me personally and for all who knew and loved him. His spirit of dedication and love of the scriptures lives on in my heart.

The night he died, Doug demonstrated the power of the scriptures in his life. His father read to him his final New Testament chapter to complete his consecutive reading goal. Most of the athletes he had cheered on in life paid reverent tribute to Doug in death as they solemnly passed by his casket and attended his funeral. We honored Doug Shaw as a seminary graduate later that May in the Ogden Tabernacle by having his parents come forward and receive his four-year seminary graduation certificate. All were touched by the spirit of that moment. Doug's spirit was truly felt.

I teach a song to my students each year to assist them in their daily scripture reading. I even give them extra-credit if they will sing it over at school . . . down the halls or in the classroom . . . in groups or alone. It's like a righteous jingle. If advertisers can use catchy jingles to sell bad things like beer, why can't we sing something that reminds us of good things—the scriptures! I learned the chorus from an inservice instructor years ago in the Ogden area and have adapted it to fit my own personality and guitar accompaniment. I sing it with original fun examples as verses but would like to share the chorus with you, for I feel the message is powerful.

> *I read my scriptures every day*
> *Scripture reading is the way*
> *To have him with me every hour*
> *I'll face the world with scripture power*

I know reminders like this help. I have been utilizing this little song for more than fifteen years now. Years after being in my class, former students will say to me, "Hey, Bro, I still remember the 'Scripture Song,'" and then they sing it. Wow, a righteous jingle with power. A reminder to *read the scriptures* every day!

ACHIEVING POWER IN THE SCRIPTURES

When you think of power, what do you think of? Maybe a 747 jumbo jet taking off, or maybe a freight train running down the track, the devastation caused by an enormous tornado, or the Internet and the ability to communicate with people all over the world?

God's words are powerful, too. His words are found in the scriptures. In the Book of Alma we read: "The word had a great tendency to lead the people to do that which was just—yea, it had had more powerful effect upon the minds of the people than the sword, or anything else, which had happened unto them—therefore Alma thought it was expedient that they should try the virtue of the word of God" (Alma 31:5).

Someone has said, "We speak to God in prayer, and he speaks to us through the scriptures."

We are reminded that "whatsoever [the General Authorities] shall speak when moved upon by the Holy Ghost shall be scripture, shall be the will of the Lord, shall be the mind of the Lord, shall be the word of the Lord, shall be the voice of the Lord, and the power of God unto salvation" (D&C 68:4). The Lord's appointed servants can reveal additional truth to the world as well as expound and clarify our present scripture.

We can also receive personal revelation. The word of the Lord can reveal truth to our souls. The late Apostle, Elder Bruce R. McConkie, has said: "I cannot use any language that describes to you what revelation is. Somebody said, 'How can I tell if I have had a revelation? I have had a feeling that such and such is true. How can I be sure?' Revelation is not something that you describe. Revelation is something that you experience" ("Personal Revelation" [address delivered to the Salt Lake Institute of Religion, 22 January 1971], 7).

I remember a critical time in my life when I "experienced revelation" from the Lord. It was when I was a freshman at Dixie College. I had just finished a successful football season under then first-year coach, Lee Bunnell. One Sunday, while attending my college ward sacrament meeting, I heard the homecoming mission report of Elder Dan Bundy who had served his mission in New York. As he spoke of his experience and bore his strong witness of service to the Lord, the Spirit testified to my soul that I needed to serve a mission. I had always planned on serving a mission. My patriarchal blessing confirmed the need as well. But I guess I just needed to find out for myself. The Spirit was working in my heart. I carried it home with me to my room. I found myself on my knees praying longer and harder than I had ever previously done. I was humbled. I really wanted to receive that spiritual confirmation for myself. I was concerned about leaving my college football and tennis scholarships, . . . about leaving my girlfriend. You know, the same kinds of things all young men worry about when deciding to serve a mission. A strong impression came into my heart after this special conversation with the Lord: "I, the Lord, am bound when ye do what I say; but when ye do not what I say, ye have no promise." It was not until I was in the

Language Training Center (LTM), now the Missionary Training Center (MTC), that I found out where this was located . . . in the Doctrine and Covenants, section 82, verse 10. From this experience, I knew everything would be all right. I did not need to worry. If football and tennis were still on the agenda after my mission, then the scholarships would still be there. And if it was right that my relationship with my girlfriend continue after I returned, then it would also continue. I simply needed to "do HIS will." The blessings would follow.

SCRIPTURE UNDERSTANDING COMES WITH FAITH, DILIGENCE, AND MEDITATION

Learning to study the scriptures is much like learning to ride a unicycle . . . it does not just happen overnight. It takes lots of practice. I received my unicycle for Christmas when I was thirteen years old. Several weeks and many spills later, seated on a torn and taped unicycle seat, I had my perseverance finally rewarded; . . . I could actually balance on and ride my unicycle. However, just looking at the unicycle and wishing I could ride it wouldn't have gotten it done. It took practice, practice, and more practice. Scripture understanding comes to us in much the same way. As we practice reading, we gradually become proficient at understanding the language of the scriptures. But it takes faith, diligence, and meditation to reach our goal.

An example of faith and diligence is found in the following story. One of my ninth-grade seminary students at Roy Junior High School was having a difficult time understanding the Old Testament, so she had stopped reading. I was in a position to counsel her one day after class, and I prayed for inspiration. I knew Heavenly Father wants us all to feel the power of the scriptures. I did not think she was an exception. I promised her if she would humbly approach her Heavenly Father in prayer and ask for his help in understanding that which she read, she would receive his divine guidance. The answer and application seemed so simple. She was so excited to tell me about her experience, she came over to the seminary before school, and I was pleased to hear of her "little miracle." "Brother Nelson, I prayed and I understood the scriptures for the first time!" Lori's faith and diligence were rewarded. "Whoso readeth, let him understand; he that hath the scriptures, let him search them" (3 Nephi 10:14).

Meditation or pondering is a key to understanding the scriptures and feeling their power. For example, desiring to know the things that his father had seen and believing that the Lord was able to make them known unto him, Nephi said, "I sat *pondering* in mine heart." The result of his pondering and meditation was the blessing of receiving the same vision of the tree of life that his father, Lehi, had received (see 1 Nephi 11; emphasis added).

The Prophet Joseph Smith and Sidney Rigdon had a similar experience in February, 1832, at Hiram, Ohio. While translating the Bible, they were pondering the resurrection of the dead mentioned in John 5:29. "And while we *meditated* upon these things, the Lord touched the eyes of our understandings and they were opened, and the glory of the Lord shone round about" (D&C 76:15–18; emphasis added). What was the result? The great revelation on the three degrees of glory—section 76!

Similarly, President Joseph F. Smith received a vision of the redemption of the dead: "I sat in my room *pondering* over the scriptures; and reflecting upon the great atoning sacrifice . . . [and] the eyes of my understanding were opened, and the Spirit of the Lord rested upon me, and I saw the hosts of the dead, both small and great" (D&C 138:1, 11; emphasis added).

Now I am *not* suggesting that all of us will have visions as a result of our pondering and meditating on the scriptures, but I testify to you the Lord will direct, prompt, encourage, enlighten, and bless you in personal ways. Personal revelation does come from the word of the Lord. I testify that the scriptures are as valuable to us as the *Liahona* was to Lehi's family. The scriptures, like the "pointers," "work according to the faith and diligence and heed which we did give unto them" (1 Nephi 16:28). The scriptures are the iron rod, the word of God, which will safely guide us through (see 1 Nephi 15:23–25; *Hymns*, no. 274).

After testifying of the enormous effort expended to bring forth the new Latter-day Saint edition of the Bible, the Book of Mormon, Doctrine and Covenants, and Pearl of Great Price, Elder Boyd K. Packer said, "They [the stick of Judah and the stick of Joseph] are indeed one in our hands. Ezekiel's prophecy now stands fulfilled [see Ezekiel 37:15–19]. With the passing of years, these scriptures will produce successive generations of faithful Christians who know the Lord Jesus Christ and are disposed to obey His will. The older generation has been raised without them, but there is another generation growing up. The revelations will be opened to them as to no other in the history of the world. . . . They will develop a gospel scholarship beyond that which their forebears could achieve. They will have the testimony that Jesus is the Christ and be competent to proclaim Him and to defend Him" *(Ensign,* November 1982, 53).

YOU are that generation of youth of which he speaks. I pray each of you will face each day with **Scripture Power!**

Gary Nelson teaches seminary at Dixie High School in St. George, Utah. A popular youth and motivational speaker, he has been associated with EFY and CES youth/adult programs for many years. He received his bachelor's degree from Southern Utah University in business education and a master's degree from BYU in education administration. Gary is a former high school and collegiate football and tennis player who maintains an interest in all sports. He has been a sports writer for two local papers. In addition to writing and speaking, he enjoys hunting, fishing, camping, bodysurfing, scuba diving, singing, playing the piano and guitar, and spending time with his family. He is a member of the high council and the Young Men presidency in his stake. Gary and his wife, Christine, are the parents of seven children.

19

REMEMBER TO FLY!

Steve Adams

One of the most cherished experiences of my life was serving as an EFY counselor for four years. I loved it when participants from previous years would return for another session. It was inspiring to see how they had grown and to sense their incredible commitment to covenants, commandments, and cleanliness. Seeing them and feeling their spirit strengthened my testimony of our Heavenly Father's marvelous Plan of Happiness.

However, as I visited with the wonderful youth who were returning to EFY for their second or third time, I was disturbed by something they would frequently say: "I am so glad to be back at EFY so that I can feel the Spirit again. It's been a year since I last felt the Spirit." Perhaps I should have been flattered by such devotion to the program. Perhaps I should have enjoyed the appreciation and gratitude expressed by the youth. But that was not the case.

Although EFY is a wonderful program and provides an environment where participants feel the Spirit in amplified quantities, the founders of EFY never intended that those who come would only feel the Spirit once a year. One of the aims of EFY is to teach young people how to feel and to recognize the influence of the Spirit in their lives on a *daily* basis, wherever they might be, rather than merely once every twelve months.

Perhaps I can illustrate this point by relating a short parable. It seems that a flock of turkeys had decided to come together and hold a special conference for the purpose of improving themselves. The well-organized conference offered all kinds of workshops, on every possible subject that would improve and enhance the life of a turkey.

While there was much to see and do at the conference, the "big event," the one that drew the most attention, was held over to the end of the conference. It was the anticipation of this final program that caused so many of the big birds to gather in such large numbers. The organizers were bringing in a "turkey guru" to teach all of these domesticated, flightless fowls how to fly! They were so excited they could hardly contain themselves. What a treat it would be to see the world from such a new and exciting perspective!

As promised, the guru taught the turkeys how to fly. The skies were soon filled with turkeys. They were having the time of their lives, leaving the ground far below and soaring up with the other birds. They enjoyed the exhilarating speed and freedom as they raced from place to place. They dive-bombed each other and honed their flying skills with each practice flight. Their masterful teacher had given them a whole new perspective on life.

At last the conference came to an end. All of the turkeys were saddened to have to leave their new friends and acquaintances—with whom they had learned so much— to return to their normal lives. Then, as the tearful good-byes ensued, and it came time for them to leave, all of the turkeys proceeded to *walk* home.

Consider for a moment the implications of this story. Why did the turkeys decide to walk home when they had all learned how to fly? They knew the principles of flight. They had practiced the techniques. They knew the benefits, joy, and happiness that they had experienced and how flying could continue to bless their lives. Yet, they left all of their training and experiences behind, and *walked* out the door!

The parallels between EFY and the Great Turkey Conference are easy to see. Are we any different from the turkeys if we learn to fly spiritually during our time at EFY, youth conferences, girls camp, or other such Church programs, and then "walk home"? Are we any different if we fail to apply the things the Spirit taught each of us during those experiences? Are we any different if we don't see a change in our daily lives? Did those experiences really do us any good if we return home and fail to follow up on the impressions that we received while at the conference?

Elder Albert E. Bowen, a member of the Quorum of the Twelve Apostles, once said: "Men are mortal and beset by human frailties. . . . When they are under the influence of an exalted occasion, they make high resolves. They firmly determine to avoid past mistakes and to do better. But gone out from under the spell of that influence and absorbed in the complicated pursuits of life, they find difficulty in holding fast to their noble purposes. . . . So it is essential that they come again, and frequently, under the influence which kindles anew the warmth of spirit in which good resolutions are begotten, that they may go out fortified to withstand the pressures of temptation which lure them into false ways" (in Conference Report, October 1949, 139).

A colleague and coordinator at EFY used to compare the EFY experience to a huge "spiritual Twinkie." Now don't misunderstand me. I love Twinkies. They make a wonderful "pick-me-up" snack. But if all we ever ate for breakfast, lunch, dinner, and every snack was Twinkies, what would happen? Can you imagine the weight that you would put on? Can you imagine stuffing yourselves with those delicious, cream-filled cakes until that same filling had replaced the blood in your veins? Again, I ask, what would happen? You would die! Probably explode! What an ugly thought—death by Twinkie!

If you were to replace the fruit, vegetables, grains, cereal, and dairy and meat products you ought to eat, with a diet of Twinkies, you would be in serious trouble! The same thing happens to you spiritually if you come to depend on youth conferences or firesides for all your spiritual nourishment. It is essential to remember the "meat and potatoes" of the gospel as well, and to feast at the Lord's bounteous spiritual smorgasbord in this life. Don't merely "pig out" at the dessert bar. The basics of a well-balanced spiritual diet include saying your daily prayers, providing service to others, studying your scriptures, magnifying your callings, and attending your Church meetings.

It is important to keep a proper perspective on everything in the Church, and balance is a key element in our lives. One of the things we admire about the Savior is his ability to keep a perfect balance in his life—intellectually, physically, spiritually, and socially. A scripture in Luke—the only one we have describing his teenage years—teaches this concept so well: "And Jesus increased in *wisdom* and *stature,* and in *favour with God* and *man*"(Luke 2:52; emphasis added).

If the pendulum swings way out to the lazy, non-committed side, we are dangerously out of balance. On the other hand, if we swing to the opposite side of the spectrum and become fanatical about everything, we are likewise way out of balance. We must be diligent, committed, and enduring to gain the prize (see 2 Nephi 31:19–21).

Another mistake we can make is to compare the various programs of the Church to each other—expecting them all to be the same. For example, after an intense week of activities at EFY, some participants, upon returning home, complain that "seminary is not like EFY." This is a true statement, but they are not meant to be like each other! True, the purpose of each is to assist in bringing young people to Christ, but the methods used to do so are quite different. The EFY program is a one-week, intense experience, while seminary lasts a full school year. Seminary's thrust is to be a constant reminder to remain faithful while living in the "real" world. On the other hand, EFY is more like a spiritual haven where you are taken "out of the world" and dropped into an atmosphere of total encouragement and concentrated learning that lasts only a week. Each program has tremendous value, but to compare them is like attempting to equate apples and oranges. It is important to recognize and appreciate the value of each—without trying to compare them.

Perhaps I can illustrate better through a hobby of mine: golf. A professional golfer is allowed to carry only fourteen clubs in his bag. Each club is designed to fulfill a different but specific purpose. The driver is designed in such a way as to gain maximum distance off the tee. On the surface it may seem to be the "hero" club because it has the potential to launch the ball the farthest. The various irons are designed to enable the golfer to hit the ball a specific distance in order to land the ball on the green. This distance built into each club ranges from 250 yards to a few feet. Then there is a putter, which is only used to propel the ball a few feet at a time, but whose job is no less important than that of the driver.

Great professional golfers such as Tiger Woods, Jack Nicklaus, or Arnold Palmer have learned to make maximum and skillful use of each club in their quest, which is to shoot the lowest possible score and win golf tournaments. They recognize the value of each club. They neither compare them, nor do they expect one club to serve equally well in all situations.

As Church members, in order to be the best that we can be, we should be grateful for each of the programs of the Church and respect and appreciate how each is unique, individual, and important. Each program is not of equal value, so we must remember to prioritize them in our lives according to the teachings of the scriptures, our Church leaders, and the inspiration of the Holy Ghost. By so doing, we will gain the maximum benefit from each Church program in *our* quest, which is to get back to our Heavenly Father, through His Son, Jesus Christ—so that we may live with them forever.

A frequently heard comment at the end of an EFY session is phrased something like, "I loved how I felt this week." What a great expression! But it is important that you know what it was that you felt, and who it was that made you feel that way. You need to recognize that those feelings are from the Holy Ghost. The scriptures tell us that the fruits of the Spirit are "love, joy, peace, longsuffering, gentleness, goodness, faith, meekness, [and] temperance" (Galatians 5:22–23). It is the Holy Ghost who is responsible for those feelings, not any one program (see D&C 8:2–3; John 15:26; John 14:26; Moroni 10:3–5).

We love to be at EFY because it is like attending a little "Mormon Disneyland." It is all *positive* peer pressure. Temptation is almost nonexistent. We are constantly being encouraged to do and be better. We build each other, read scriptures, learn principles, and study doctrines that help us better understand and live the gospel. We pray together, serve others, and leave "the world" behind. It is a veritable little utopian society.

The key to the entire experience at EFY is to learn all you can and then **take it all home with you!** If you always want to feel the way you do while at EFY, then do the things that you do while you are here! One caution to bear in mind, however, is that you cannot *force* the Spirit. It simply cannot be done. But you can create an environment conducive to the Spirit and do the things that will invite the Spirit to be there with you. I cannot overemphasize the idea that *if you want to feel the way that you feel at EFY, you must continue to do the things that you do while you are here.*

The following is a partial list of things that you could continue doing in order to enjoy the same blessings and spirit that you have felt during your EFY experience:

1. Prayer. Begin and end each day in conversation with your Father in Heaven. It should go without saying that it is also important to take advantage of this opportunity at any other time you feel the impression to pray (see Alma 34:18–27; Alma 37:36–37; 2 Nephi 32:8–9).

2. Scripture study. Set aside a time to study your scriptures on a daily basis (and do not let another day of your life go by without supping from those precious pages).

Read at the same time every day, and it will become a habit that you will be eternally grateful that you began (see Joshua 1:8–9; 1 Nephi 19:23; Alma 17:2–3).

3. Attend church. Do not miss your Church meetings. That is where you recharge your spiritual batteries on a weekly basis—particularly during the sacrament (see Moroni 6:5–6; D&C 6:32; Mosiah 18:25).

4. Attend seminary. Be a four-year graduate! Learn the mastery scriptures. Study the word of the Lord, and it will help you not only to prepare yourself to be a better missionary but will also assist you in being a better marriage partner (see D&C 88:63, 83; D&C 112:10; 1 Nephi 3:7).

5. Serve others. The best cure for depression is service—and the opportunities to serve are endless if you look for them (see Matthew 16:24–26; 25:40; Mosiah 2:17).

6. Good friends. Associate with those who share your same values and standards. Lift, build, and encourage one another to be the best you can be (see John 15:13; 2 Nephi 1:30; Proverbs 17:17).

7. Uplifting music. This can be a powerful source of goodness and strength, or it can produce the opposite effects. Satan also knows the power of music, and he uses it to degrade, desensitize, and destroy. Listen to good music; avoid that which is offensive to the Spirit (see D&C 25:12; Psalm 96:1; D&C 136:28).

8. Media. Be aware of how much and what type of media you consume (e.g. movies, videos, magazines, books, etc.). Follow the standards set forth in the pamphlet *For the Strength of Youth.*

9. Follow the Brethren. What a privilege we enjoy—living in this day and age! We are blessed with frequent opportunities to see and listen to a living prophet and divinely inspired apostles. No other generation has had such access to them and their teachings. In fact, for nearly two thousand years following the death of Christ, the world stumbled about in the darkness, vainly looking for the light (see D&C 1:37–38; Amos 3:7; D&C 21:4–6).

10. Repent. This is such a beautiful principle! We need

to apply it in our lives on a daily basis. I wish that I could report that since the day of my baptism at age eight, during at least one day in my life, I have had no need to repent. But such is not the case. How grateful I am for the Savior's atonement and for his invitation to come unto him (see Matthew 11:28–30; D&C 18:10–13; Mosiah 26:30; D&C 58:42–43). (I hope that you will take the time to look up each of the scriptures referenced in this chapter!)

Though these may seem like simple suggestions, I know they can make an incredible difference in a person's life. Because of the profound impact they have had in my life, I know that these principles are true. Power in the gospel comes not so much by doing the great, marvelous, and heroic feats, but simply by having the strength and courage to do the simple things on a consistent, daily basis.

It is my hope and fervent prayer that you and I will take the spirit of EFY home; that we will do those things that will enable us to have the Holy Spirit as our constant companion; that we will recognize his influence in our lives—on a *daily* basis—and not just annually. Now that we have learned how to "fly," let us soar with the eagles, rather than remaining earthbound with the turkeys (see Isaiah 40:31). Let's make each day a little "EFY on Earth!"

Steve Adams was born and reared in Salt Lake City, Utah. He served a mission in the Washington Spokane Spanish-Speaking Mission. He taught seminary for six years in the Salt Lake area and is now teaching religion at BYU and pursuing a Ph.D. in sociology. Steve met his beautiful wife, Deanne Pope Adams, in 1991, while they were both counselors at EFY. Needless to say, they both love EFY a lot. They have the two cutest little boys in the whole world: Matt and Sam. Steve loves all outdoor activities, especially hiking, camping, fishing, and hunting. This is Steve's eleventh year working with Especially for Youth and Outreach youth conferences.

20

BECOMING
A ZION PEOPLE

Allen Litchfield

When I was a small child, my family lived in Alberta, Canada, but every summer vacation we would drive to Sandy, Utah, to spend a few weeks visiting my grandmother. My mother, who had grown up in Sandy, would talk about "going down to Zion." So, while my friends would spend part of their summer holidays at Disneyland or camping somewhere, we always stayed in what we called "Zion."

The weeks we spent in Sandy at Grandma's place were wonderful for the small children in our family, so when we read in family scripture study that Zion was a great place, we agreed completely. My grandmother's backyard was not like any other we were familiar with. She had several acres of ground, taken up by a huge garden, an entire orchard of fruit trees, various domesticated animals, hives of bees, and an irrigation ditch. Located across the street from her house there were also several schools, which provided playgrounds that were usually vacant in the summer. In addition, the schools supplied us with large cement and paved areas that were perfect for roller-skating. All my brothers and sisters were dedicated "skaters," long before skateboarding was invented. Each of us had a pair of clamp-on, metal-wheeled roller skates that attached to our shoes, and we spent hours every day skating around the school walks and parking lots.

We never slept in during our summer days in Zion. Because each day was so filled with wonders and joys, we did not want to waste a minute of it. We would get up early, "help" Grandma in the garden for a while, have a great breakfast, and then head outside for a full day of adventures. One summer, when I was about seven or eight, my brother Bryant and I carefully planned the last day of that particular vacation in Utah. We would be heading home the following day, so we wanted to enjoy all of our favorite activities one last time. He and I roller-skated till we could barely stand, played various sports and games with elaborate made-up rules like Calvin and Hobbes, and ate our fill of raspberries and apricots. Late in the afternoon we were sitting up in a rough tree house that we had built in a crab apple tree. I can't remember all the details of the game we were playing, but it involved "bombing" the ducks below the tree with crab apples. One of us lay back on a tree branch and said something like, "Don't you wish we could live in Zion all the time?" We agreed that living in Zion was the best and promised each other that we would move down to Zion and settle in permanently just as soon as we were old enough. The next morning we drove away from Grandma's house with the same feelings of reluctance that the early members of the Church must have felt as they left their homes and farms in Missouri or Nauvoo.

I remember sitting in a Primary class back in Canada some time later and being asked by my teacher where I thought Zion was. Without a moment's hesitation I replied that Zion was at my grandmother's house in Utah. The teacher smiled and agreed that Utah was sometimes referred to as Zion, but suggested that the term Zion sometimes also pointed to other places and ways of being. These many years later, I don't remember the other places where the teacher might have suggested Zion was, but I do remember thinking that she was wrong—that Zion was only at my grandma's house. Though I am now aware that Utah is a big place, as children we considered "Utah" and "Grandma's place" as exactly the same thing. When we said we were going to Utah, we meant Grandma's house. So when I asked my mother after Primary if Zion was in Utah, and she said it was, I felt better. I loved Grandma's place, and I was sure that there was nothing like it anywhere else. I didn't like people suggesting that there might be other Zions in various places around the world.

Now, about forty years later, my grandmother and even my mother have passed away. In Sandy, Grandma's former orchard and fields are now filled with dozens of strangers' houses. When we do drive by the area now, nothing is the way it was. One thing that hasn't changed, however, is that we and many people we know are still seeking and longing for that warm and wonderful, sunny and serene, exalted and excited Zion feeling. I think it is because that Zion feeling reminds us of our life before this one, when we lived with our Heavenly parents. Living in a "Zion condition" is the closest we can come here on earth to the way it was living with them. That is why men have always dreamed of living in a utopian or holy community and have tried to design, in theory and practice, such pure and perfect societies.

Establishing Zion has always been the ultimate ideal and goal of every prophet and community of Saints. Joseph Smith wrote in 1842 that "the building up of Zion is a cause that has interested the people of God in every age; it is a theme upon which prophets, priests and kings have dwelt with peculiar delight" (*History of the Church,* 4:609). Though the goal has always been central in every period of religious history, certain groups and eras have come closer than others to reaching this goal. Enoch and his people were so successful in establishing Zion that their city was taken into heaven (see Moses 7:23). Following the resurrection of the Savior, the Saints in New Testament times made an attempt to establish Zion: "And all that believed were together, and had all things common" (Acts 2:44). After the visit of the risen Lord to the people of the Book of Mormon, "the people were all converted unto the Lord, . . . and there were no contentions and disputations among them, and every man did deal justly one with another. And they had all things common among them; therefore there were not rich and poor, bond and free, but they were all made free, and partakers of the heavenly gift" (4 Nephi 1:2–3). This blessed condition lasted almost two hundred years.

In the early days of the restoration of the gospel, the Lord spoke frequently of Zion, and the Doctrine and Covenants is sprinkled with the recurring call to "bring forth and establish the cause of Zion" (see D&C 6:6; 11:6; 12:6; 14:6). Joseph Smith taught that "We ought to have the building up of Zion as our greatest object" (*Teachings of the Prophet Joseph Smith,* 160). Building Zion is what Saints of the kingdom have always been about. If we are going to build it, we must learn what it looks like and feels like. First, though, we should understand what the term Zion means.

The name Zion is used in several ways. The Greek word probably first meant "bright, sunny place" and was often used in reference to elevated places like hills and mountains. This definition matches the childish idea we had of our grandmother's home being Zion. It was for us a bright, happy, joyful place. But the term Zion has a deeper and more profound meaning. Zion has been applied to the ancient "City of Holiness, even Zion" (JST Genesis 7:25), founded by Enoch. This city and its people were called Zion by the Lord because "they were of one heart and one mind, and dwelt in righteousness; and there was no poor among them" (Moses 7:18). This is the standard or pattern by which we measure all later attempts to establish Zion. At the time of King David, Mount Zion was the name of a hill located in the Jerusalem area and, by extension of meaning, the city of Jerusalem itself. In some scriptural contexts, Zion still refers to Jerusalem or the land of Israel.

With that Old Testament usage in mind, the Jewish colonists who gathered back to the Holy Land in the twentieth century called themselves Zionists.

The lands of the Americas are sometimes also referred to as Zion. Joseph Smith said in 1840 that the "land of Zion consists of all of North and South America." But interestingly, in the same sentence, he added that "any place where the Saints gather is Zion" (*The Words of Joseph Smith* [1980], 415). Therefore, specific places of gathering are sometimes labeled Zion. One special place of gathering is the New Jerusalem in Independence, Jackson County, Missouri (see D&C 57:1–3). This place has been significant and will continue to be so, especially during the millennial reign of our Savior. But more generally, any land of peace, refuge, gathering, and safety for the Saints of God can be considered a Zion (see D&C 45:66). It is in this sense that the place of pioneer gathering in the West—Utah and the intermountain area of the United States—is termed Zion.

Finally, and most importantly, Zion is more than a place, city, or continent—it is a condition, a state of righteous being. In this sense the Church or kingdom of God is often called Zion, using the term in a metaphorical sense and because the Lord defines Zion as "the pure in heart" (D&C 97:21). Zion, then, is the home of the faithful, the gathering place of the pure in heart, no matter where they happen to be situated.

These are all definitions or uses of the term Zion. But when Latter-day Saints talk of building Zion, we customarily aren't referring to particular efforts to build up Utah, Jerusalem, or even Missouri. The Brethren have not, for many decades, asked converts to move to Utah after joining the Church. We have not, as a people, been asked to move to Missouri. The prophets will tell us at the appropriate time when and how we should build up those specific Zion places mentioned in scripture. Instead of concerning ourselves about Jackson County, our task at the moment is to follow the counsel of our Church leaders to help build up the community of the Saints or the Church by becoming a Zion people wherever we currently reside. So until new instructions from the Lord are given, we should make it our objective to build up Zion in ourselves, our families, our wards and stakes, our schools, and our communities.

One trait of Zion is love. Zion is about people lovingly looking after each other. The Doctrine and Covenants describes Zion as "every man seeking the interest of his neighbor, and doing all things with an eye single to the glory of God" (D&C 82:19). Zion is only achieved when people are so concerned with the well-being of others that they willingly give up some of their own desires. Many years ago I enjoyed teaching two exceptional young men of Zion in one of my seminary classes. I will call them Bob and Bill. Both were handsome, bright, tall, and athletic. They tended to date pretty and popular girls but were friendly to everyone. There was also a young woman with special needs in that same class. Betty had been born with congenital birth defects that resulted in a homely appearance and learning disabilities. As the world would judge, she was extremely unattractive and slow thinking. As you might imagine, she had never had a date.

We didn't often teach lessons on dating in seminary, but, just as at EFY, the subject was popular and generated a lot of interest. The students were anxious to talk about dates they had really had, some they pretended to have had, and ones they hoped they would someday have. Betty didn't usually say very much in class, but during this spirited exchange on dating, she asked this question, "Do you think I will ever have a date?" The class grew instantly silent, and I thought for a few seconds about how I should respond. I was about to give one of those general, noncommittal answers. You know, like the ones your father always gave when you asked him for your own pony. Just then Bill and Bob spoke up. I hadn't asked them to rescue me or Betty, but they looked Betty right in the eyes and said, "We are sure you will have some dates." Over the next year or so, Bob and Bill, either together or individually, took Betty out several times. Both these outstanding young men went on to serve missions, marry, and move away, probably not realizing what a great service they had performed.

A few years ago, I met Betty again. She was by then about forty years old, still single, and living in a group home. I asked her to tell me about the last few decades of her life. She said that she hadn't done very much of anything and couldn't remember having any recent fun, but then a light came into her eyes and a smile lit up her face as she said, "Have I ever told you about my dates with Bill and Bob?" With excitement, she recounted every detail of those dates in the 1970s. I couldn't help thinking that if Betty lived in Zion, she would have had more recent social adventures but was thankful that she had known two Zion-like young men in her youth, so she could at least have those treasured memories.

A second characteristic of Zion is unity. In 1834, the Lord explained to the Saints why Zion had not yet been redeemed. He declared that they were "not united according to the union required by the law of the celestial kingdom; And Zion cannot be built up unless it is by the principles of the law of the celestial kingdom; otherwise I cannot receive her unto myself" (D&C 105:4–5). Unity is about being of one heart and one mind.

Some EFY sessions I have participated in over the years have approached that level of unity. A session at San Antonio, Texas, was so filled with unity and love that one of the campus police officers asked if he could help deliver the pizza to the various dorms on Tuesday night. He told me that he had never been involved with a similar group of young people and that he wanted an excuse to be around them. "They are like angels or teenagers from another planet," he said. The following evening the EFY youth were interacting compassionately and joyfully out on the campus football field with a group called Buddies (youth and adults from the area who had various developmental challenges and disabilities). Two women joggers stopped running to ask me who these incredible young people were. One of them commented that she knew there were some youth in the world capable of being kind, but asked, "how is it possible that every kid out there is being kind all at once?" In a different session in Virginia, years earlier, I remember that, on their own and without it being organized by the counselors, the participants decided to make sure everyone was included and involved at the closing dance. During almost every song, every single person was dancing, which was pretty amazing because of the imbalance in the ratio of girls to boys at the event. There were trios and foursomes out there dancing away, even on the slow songs.

There have been times when I have felt the Lord was holding the entire session of youth in his hands, and I was reminded of the scripture: "Behold, the land of Zion—I, the Lord, hold it in mine own hands" (D&C 63:25). It is a wonderful feeling to achieve that kind of unity during a week of EFY, but we need to do something even more difficult. Just as we are reminded by the lines of the famous EFY farewell song, we need to "take it home." Once we have tasted of Zion, we will want to experience it more often than one week out of fifty-two. We need to strive for that kind of unity in our families, wards and branches of the Church, and communities. Only by arriving at that stage of unity can we become part of Christ. He has reminded us, "I say unto you, be one; and if ye are not one ye are not mine" (D&C 38:27).

A third characteristic of Zion is purity. The Lord announced in the early days of the restored Church: "I will raise up unto myself a pure people, that will serve me in righteousness" (D&C 100:16). More recently President Kimball taught that "Zion can be built up only among those who are the pure in heart. . . . Not a people who are pure in appearance, rather people who are pure in heart. Zion is to be in the world and not of the world" (in

Conference Report, April 1978, 122). We must be different than the world if we are to establish Zion.

One of my former stake presidents related this true story to make that point. As he arrived home from a Church meeting, he was greeted by calls from his family to come downstairs and enjoy this "good, old family classic" on television. As he sat with his wife, married children, his small grandchildren, and his teenagers, several comments were made about "family movies" just not being made like this anymore. Toward the end of the show, with his four-year-old grandson asleep on his lap, he had a sickening flashback. He realized that this film, which was now accepted as family fare, was picketed at the theaters when it first came out in 1961 by his then Roman Catholic parents. In thirty years, the world had changed to the extent that a film that was once thought by good people to be unacceptable was now lauded as suitable for viewing, even by young children. The scariest thing about this example is that our values can be eroded so gradually that most of us never really notice the change that has taken place. It may not be enough to simply avoid R-rated movies; perhaps we must be more vigilant to avoid ideas and principles dressed up by the world in more mild and subtle disguises. President Marion G. Romney, a counselor in the First Presidency, said in conference about twenty years ago: "Remember that Enoch's Zion was built in a day when wickedness was as rampant as it is among us today. Among those who rejected the word of God in that day 'there were wars and bloodshed'; they were ripening in that iniquity which brought the flood" (in Conference Report, April 1976, 169). That is the world we live in. Remaining pure in that world is a daunting task, but one that is possible.

In conclusion, "Zion must increase in beauty, and in holiness; her borders must be enlarged; her stakes must be strengthened; yea, verily I say unto you, Zion must arise and put on her beautiful garments" (D&C 82:14). This will happen when we take seriously the Lord's recipe for Zion:

love, unity, and purity are at least three of the major components of the mixture. Those three virtues all go together well with Brigham Young's counsel and direction about approaching Zion: "As to the Spirit of Zion, it is in the hearts of the Saints, of those who love and serve the Lord with all their might, mind, and strength" (in *Journal of Discourses,* 2:253). May we do so, I pray.

Allen Litchfield married Gladys Gough and is the father of six children. He is also a former bishop and district president. Allen is an instructor of religion at Brigham Young University. A former bank administrator, he has served as a seminary teacher and principal and as an institute instructor and director. He enjoys reading, horseback riding, white-water rafting, and canoeing.

21

TAKING IT HOME WITH YOU

Matthew O. Richardson

I can remember, almost as if it were yesterday, scouring over a dried streambed, searching for rocks. Occasionally, my wife would shout out, "How about this one?" as she'd hold up a rock for my inspection. I would stand up, shield my eyes from the scorching sun, and squint to see the rock she had found. "No," I'd yell back. "It's too big and besides, it really doesn't look *smooth* enough." She'd toss the rock aside and continue her search. As you can tell, I was very particular about which rocks were to be included in my collection. I was looking for exactly five, round, smooth stones that would range in size somewhere between a golf ball and a tennis ball. I also insisted that the rocks must actually be found *in* the riverbed. I guess we looked pretty silly, standing in the middle of practically nowhere, searching for *special* rocks in the hot sun. Most everyone else was sitting in the shade sipping a cool drink.

I am not a rock fanatic. As a matter of fact, I rarely get excited about rocks at all. For me, rocks are rocks. But this time it was different. These rocks had to be just right because I wanted to take them home with me. I wanted to have something that was representative of my experience, a *souvenir* of sorts. It wasn't that I didn't have rocks back home. We have millions of rocks where I live, but we didn't have rocks that came from the Valley of Elah. You see, my wife and I had spent the afternoon at the very location attributed in the scriptures as the place where David first met Goliath (not only was it their first meeting, but it was also their last!). I know you are familiar with the story. It was in a streambed in this very valley that David found "five smooth stones" (1 Samuel 17:40) and used one of them to dispose of Israel's gigantic enemy. I have always loved that story, and to stand in the place where it actually happened was something that I didn't want to forget. In my simple reasoning, I figured that five smooth stones would serve to keep my memories of this experience fresh. In a way, I guess I was right. After all these years, those stones still remind me of a hot sunny afternoon my wife and I spent together in Elah.

We all have experiences that we wish would never end. Unfortunately, as the cliché accurately predicts: "All things must come to an end." While every event surely passes, I believe that it doesn't really have to end. I have discovered you can stretch an experience into years and make those memories just as real and sweet as when the event first occurred. There are ways, if persons truly desire, to take the experience home with them and allow it to have a significant impact upon their life: both today and forever. May I offer three simple suggestions of how we can prolong events by taking them home with us and thus making them part of us.

REVIEW

Not long ago, I gave a talk where I used several personal experiences to illustrate a principle. After the presentation was over, I talked with some of those who were in attendance. One person made a comment that I must have an exciting life to have so many experiences. I told them that I probably hadn't had any more experiences than the next person, but that I was perhaps just better able to remember my experiences. To this they replied, "Then you must have an amazing memory!" I sincerely believe that while my memory is adequate, it is far from amazing. For me, there is a trick to remembering things. It all begins with reviewing.

Reviewing an experience is different than remembering an event. In fact, reviewing is an important process that actually precedes remembering. Reviewing is something that must be done while the experience is still fresh in your mind and in your heart. In some ways, it doesn't require a good memory to review. It has been said that the secret of a good memory is attention. I believe this to be true. By reviewing something, you pay attention to the details while they are still fresh in your mind. Since the experience is fresh, your energy is used to sort events out, think of lessons learned, and review impressions and feelings.

Some people review their experiences by keeping a journal. They record events in detail almost as soon as they transpire. This provides a lasting review of an experience. Since a good review is more than a mere accounting of an experience, a journal can be used to record more than the easy-to-remember facts. President Spencer W. Kimball encouraged each of us to record "your goings and comings, your deepest thoughts, your achievements and your failures, your associations and your triumphs, your impressions and your testimonies" (*The Teachings of Spencer W. Kimball* [1982], 351). If you don't keep a journal, at least outline the significant experiences you have while they are still fresh in both your mind and your heart. There might be some experiences that you still hold close to your heart even though they happened some time ago. If you want to retain those memories and prolong them into lifelong experiences, you should review what is left and record all the details you can.

Another helpful thing is to gather and save objects that will remind you of the experience. Obviously, this must be done during and soon afterward. Tangible objects provide a good way of reviewing significant events. They provide a map, of sorts, to recall the details of an experience. There are those who save everything from ticket stubs to ribbons, napkins to pictures, or even rocks, as a way of preserving memories. Some organize their mementos in a scrapbook, while others may hang items on their walls or display them on a self. If you collect *things,* make sure that they are more than just *things.* Save only those items that spark the memories worth remembering. My home is filled with objects that have significant value. Not necessarily monetary value, mind you, but a priceless value for my family and me. Almost every object in my home reminds me of landmark events.

Perhaps the most common way to review your experience is to talk about it. Tell someone else what you did, who was there, and how you felt. Have you ever talked with someone who has just recently returned from Especially for Youth, a newly returned missionary, or someone who was just married? What is the topic of their conversation? It is their experiences! Have you noticed that they talk about their experience without a pause, almost without breathing? Ask a newly returned missionary about his mission experience. You will hear more about Denmark (or wherever he served), baptisms, companions, dogs, bad meals, tracting, frustrations, conjugating verbs, and the mysteries of the scriptures than you ever cared to know. I am amazed at the detail, emotion, and clarity that characterize such accounts. These people aren't simply remembering an event, they are literally reviewing that experience (sometimes the *whole* experience) with you.

If you really want to *take* an experience *home with* you, you must have something to take. Reviewing your experience, by whatever means you choose, will help you retain the memory permanently. But if you rely upon memory alone, details of the experience quickly begin to fade. It is only a matter of time before the substance of your experience is gone, leaving you only a skeleton remembrance of what happened.

RETURN

Some of the most significant things that happen to us may literally be "once in a lifetime" events. C. S. Lewis once wrote: "Why is it that one can never think of the past without wanting to go back?" (*The Letters of C. S. Lewis to Arthur Greeves: 1914–1963* [1986], 87). This yearning to return to meaningful experiences and events is another key to making an experience part of you. While we cannot literally return to the past, we can return in other ways.

When you have a valuable experience, I hope you will look for opportunities to duplicate it, if possible. You may have the chance to go to another session of Especially for Youth next year, or revisit special friends, or return to a favorite location. Though it won't be the exact same experience, it could provide similar happenings that will continue to nudge you down the same path.

If you can't literally return to an event or repeat it, then return to those things that made that experience memorable. You can return to an experience by actually doing some of the things that you did *during* the memorable experience. Granted you can't go to workshops, hold a dance on your own, or knock on all the doors of your neighborhood and share the gospel message. Significant experiences, however, are more than just events. The best part of your experience, whether you realized it or not, is what the event reflected, not the activity itself. For example, I have fond memories of the fun experiences I had with my wife prior to our marriage. We laughed, had long talks, walked hand in hand, and were in love. When I think back, I can remember many good experiences we shared. In some ways, I still long for those days. We have been married for many years, and it is literally impossible to return to earlier times and relive the exact events. But we can return by doing the kinds of things we did in those early years. It wasn't the specific dance (or whatever event) that was important, it was being and growing together. That is why my wife and I still go on dates, laugh, have long talks, walk hand in hand—in an effort to keep our love alive and growing. We return as often as we can to those things that originally brought us together. Therefore, while you may not be able to literally return to EFY, the mission field, a family event, or a fond experience, return to the elements that made those experiences significant. Say your prayers, seek spiritual experiences, listen to uplifting words, talk with friends from the adventure, live as you lived while you were there.

Never underestimate the power of the mind to retain the things we see, feel, taste, smell, and hear. President Benson reminded us that, "It is our privilege to store our memories with good and great thoughts and bring them out on the stage of our minds at will" (*The Teachings of Ezra Taft Benson* [1988], 382). Take my visit to Elah, for example. I haven't had the opportunity to return there in person, but I can't count the number of times I have gone back to that dry streambed in my mind. What a blessing our mind becomes. In the same way, I have returned to many Scout camps, family vacations, the mission field, the occasion on which I met my wife for the first time, delivery rooms, funny situations, and those times that have warmed my heart. I feel lucky to be able to revisit these places and to do it as often as I wish. Another benefit is that the more often you return to your experience, the more it becomes part of you.

The objects we have gathered sometimes invite us to return when we least expect it. After a long day or a discouraging experience, your mood can be altered by a glimpse of something that reminds you of a great experience. It is amazing how quickly a picture, program, name tag, ribbon, autograph, familiar scripture, souvenir, a note or letter, or just about anything else can trigger a flood of memories. Great memories await those who surround themselves with helpful reminders. Remember my rocks?

Whenever I look at them, I am reminded of the time my wife and I spent one sunny afternoon in Elah. Those rocks, however, remind me of *more* than that. They make me think of the story of David and of his courage. I also think of the commitments I made in the valley to exhibit similar courage when I was faced with my own Goliaths. I am also reminded of how I carried a very heavy suitcase, filled with rocks, through other countries and how custom officials looked at me as though I was weird as they inspected my bags. My rocks, like all objects backed with fond memories and meanings, are not mere souvenirs, they are important reminders of important lessons. I originally hoped to bring a part of Elah home with me in the form of rocks. In reality, I was lucky enough to find Elah, not only in the rocks but in me as well.

Finally, there's one other element that makes it possible to recall our past experiences more vividly—the power of the Spirit. As we review the spiritual, life-changing events of our lives, the Holy Ghost not only brings these things to our remembrance, but permits us to experience our original feelings again. This is a wonderful gift. Referring to the time when the Nephites were originally converted, Alma sought to reinforce their faith by asking them to recall the emotion they had felt at that time: "And now behold, I say unto you, my brethren, if ye have experienced a change of heart, and if ye have felt to sing the song of redeeming love, I would ask, *can you feel so now?*" (Alma 5:26; emphasis added). Therefore, the next time you return to the events that have made impact upon you, make sure you get the full impact. Whether you are returning for the second, third, or fiftieth time, breathe in the full experience. If you are living worthy of the Holy Ghost, you will be able to not only remember, but feel as you once felt. You will be spiritually recharged and enriched, and the memory will be even more deeply etched in your mind and in your heart.

REVISE

As you *review* and *return* to the significant experiences in your life, you will probably discover what I have. The experiences we have that are most important are those that cause the greatest change in our lives. There is a difference between events that are merely fun and those that are spiritually significant. Any experience that does not create a desire to make a personal change, quickly becomes one of the many events that blends into the sea of the ordinary and is soon forgotten.

I can remember a time when I received a specific answer to an earnest prayer. It was a fantastic experience that is far too personal to detail here, but it was something that altered my outlook on life. I had thought I fully understood the power of prayer, but after reviewing what happened to me, I came to the conclusion that I not only needed to continue saying my prayers, but needed to be more faithful, obedient, and dependent upon the Lord.

When an experience is so powerful that it causes us to adjust our attitudes, characteristics, or behavior, it actually contributes to the making of a *new* life. In some cases, the adjustments are so extensive they constitute a complete overhaul. Alma the younger, Paul the Apostle, and Peter the chief Apostle each had such an experience—a spiritual awakening that changed them forever. Depending on the strength of your spiritual experiences, you may need only to fine-tune your outlook, or you may have to make a more drastic change in your thoughts, habits, activities, or even your group of friends. Making the necessary revisions, whether great or small, is one of the most powerful keys to taking an experience home with you. The power is no longer the event, but it is you! In reality, this is the difference between taking something home *with* you and taking something home *in* you.

As you revise your life accordingly, you become something—something better. I love to hear parents, friends, participants, and teachers describe how much someone has changed after experiencing EFY, a mission, marriage, or other significant event in their life. This is the best way to extend any experience. This is the only way to take something home with us. Wherever you call home, you will always find one thing that is constant there—you! It is my hope that you will always take your experiences home with you by taking them home in you.

Matthew Richardson is an assistant professor at Brigham Young University in the Department of Church History and Doctrine. He served a mission to Denmark and holds a doctoral degree in Educational Leadership. Matt serves as a bishop and enjoys sports, traveling, and making Mickey Mouse pancakes on Saturday mornings. He and his wife, Lisa, have four children.